OECD Public Governance Reviews

Integrity Review of Public Procurement in Quebec, Canada

A STRATEGIC APPROACH TO CORRUPTION RISKS

Please cite this publication as:
OECD (2020), *Integrity Review of Public Procurement in Quebec, Canada: A Strategic Approach to Corruption Risks*, OECD Public Governance Reviews, OECD Publishing, Paris, *https://doi.org/10.1787/g2g95000-en*.

ISBN 978-92-64-30593-9 (print)
ISBN 978-92-64-30592-2 (pdf)

OECD Public Governance Reviews
ISSN 2219-0406 (print)
ISSN 2219-0414 (online)

Photo credits: Cover © R.M. Nunes/Shutterstock.com.

Corrigenda to publications may be found on line at: *www.oecd.org/about/publishing/corrigenda.htm*.

Foreword

Public procurement is a critical sector for achieving various public policy objectives, but it is highly vulnerable to the risk of bribery or ethical abuses. In addition to the volume of transactions and the financial interests at stake, the risks of corruption are exacerbated by the complexity of the processes, the close interaction between public officials and businesses, and the multitude of stakeholders.

Sub-national authorities are particularly vulnerable to bribery in public procurement since the share of procurement at the sub-national level accounts for 63% of public procurement in OECD countries. In Canada, almost 90% of public procurement is administered by governments at the sub-national level. It is difficult to establish with certainty the exact cost of corruption in public procurement, given the hidden nature of corruption. However, in construction projects alone, estimates of losses of between 20% and 30% of project value due to bribery are relatively widespread.

In Quebec, the extent of the corruption schemes exposed before the *Commission of Inquiry on the Awarding and Management of Public Contracts in the Construction Industry* (the Charbonneau Commission) has greatly shaken the public's confidence in its government institutions. The crisis of confidence caused by the use of public procurement for the benefit of private interests is still being felt today, which is why procurement integrity has become a major issue in Quebec. The government has put in place many robust measures in response to the recommendations of the Charbonneau Commission. Integrating them into a strategic approach to strengthen integrity and efficiency in all public procurement could make them even more effective.

According to the *Edelman* Trust Barometer, people's confidence in their government reached 55% in 2019, up 11 points from 2018 and 16 points from 2017. However, in 2018, 43% of the Quebec population estimated that government institutions are the most fragile.

Thus, a firm and unequivocal commitment to promoting the resilience of public procurement processes is needed to restore citizen trust. The Government of Quebec is fully aware of this situation, and it is in this context that it has reached out to the OECD to help it benchmark the scope of its efforts to strengthen integrity in public procurement against best practices implemented in OECD member countries. The first purpose of this integrity review is to take note of the efforts undertaken by the Government of Quebec. Second, this report discusses best practices implemented in OECD countries to strengthen integrity in public procurement that could be adapted to the Quebec context.

Despite the public outrage that the revelations of the Charbonneau Commission had caused, the Government of Quebec can seize this opportunity to mobilise all stakeholders towards achieving standards of transparency, accountability and integrity in the conduct of public procurement that compare favourably at the global level. By implementing the recommendations of this integrity review, Quebec could lay the groundwork for a strategic and proactive approach to strengthening integrity in public procurement. Ultimately, this approach could serve as a springboard for the development of a comprehensive strategy to combat corruption and strengthen integrity arrangements applicable to the civil service as a whole.

This document was approved by the OECD Working Party of Senior Public Integrity Officials (SPIO) on 6 July 2020 and the OECD Working Party of the Leading Practitioners on Public Procurement (LPP) on 31 October 2019.

This document [GOV/PGC/INT(2020)4/REV1] was approved by the Public Governance Committee on 24 September 2020 and prepared for publication by the OECD Secretariat.

Acknowledgements

This report was drafted by the Public Sector Integrity Division of the Public Governance Directorate of the OECD. Frédéric St-Martin and Frédéric Boehm co-ordinated the drafting of the report under the supervision of Janós Bertók and Julio Bacio Terracino. The chapters were written by Frédéric St-Martin, Matthieu Cahen and Kenza Khachani, with valuable contributions from Antoine Comps and Pauline Bertrand. The report was prepared for publication by Meral Gedik, Thibaut Gigou and Laura McDonald, with administrative support provided by Alpha Zambou.

The OECD expresses its gratitude to the representatives of Quebec government ministries and institutions involved in this Integrity Review of Public Procurement in Quebec who took part in the discussions organised as part of the fact-finding mission that took place from 9 to 13 July 2018 in Quebec City and Montreal: Ms Carole Arav, Mr Éric Bergeron, Ms Julie Veillette, Mr Bruno Doutriaux, Ms Sylvie Gauvin, Mr Pierre Dallaire, Ms Caroline Lortie, Mr Oliver Dumas, Mr Michel Dumont, Ms Nathalie Gosselin and Mr Philippe Bettez Quessy of the Treasury Board Secretariat; Mr Michel Duchesne and Ms Nathalie Jacques of the Ministry of Municipal Affairs and Housing; Mr Sylvain Lepage and Mr Patrick Émond of the Fédération québécoise des municipalités; Mr Éric Drouin, Mr Nicolas Fournier and Mr Jonathan Bélanger of the Ministry of Transportation, Sustainable Mobility and Transport Electrification; Mr Alain Fortin and Ms Moïsette Fortin of the Office of the Auditor General of Quebec; Mr Frédéric Pérodeau and Mr Louis Letellier of the Autorité des marchés financiers; Ms Maha Ben Salah and Ms Tabita Nicolaica of the Ministry of Labour, Employment and Social Solidarity; Mr Ghislain Arseneault of the Régie de l'Assurance maladie du Québec; Ms Caroline Fontaine of the Société québécoise des infrastructures; Mr Pierre Hamel of the Association de la construction du Québec; Mr André Rainville of the Association des firmes de génie-conseil; Ms Manon Bertrand, chairman of Construction SRB; Mr Pierre-Olivier Brodeur of the Charbonneau Commission Public Monitoring Committee; Mr Pierre-Yves Boivin and Mr Philippe Noël of the Fédération des Chambres de commerce du Québec; Ms Isabelle Jodoin of Stantec; Ms Isabelle Gagnon of Roche Diagnostics; Mr Gaëtan Demers of WSP; Mr Jasmin Savard and Ms Charlotte Deslauriers-Goulet of the Union des municipalités du Québec; Mr Benoît Pinet of the Unité permanente anticorruption; and Mr Pierre Egesborg and Mr Freddy Foley of the Office of the Inspector General of Ville de Montréal.

Table of contents

Foreword 3

Acknowledgements 5

Abbreviations and acronyms 9

Executive summary 13

1 Strengthening Integrity in Public procurement in Quebec 15

Developing an integrated institutional framework to implement a coherent approach to integrity across government and municipalities 16
Defining values and standards of integrity and applying them to specific contexts 21
Risk management and optimal controls to strengthen prevention and accountability 26
References 32

2 A strategic definition of the needs of public actors in Quebec 33

Objective, transparent and politically independent planning of works and infrastructure projects 35
Strengthening the integrity of public procurement by strengthening and harmonising planning processes 39
References 46
Note 47

3 The use of competitive public procurement in Quebec 49

Towards the use of appropriate contract management procedures 50
Using selection and award criteria that prevent bribery and bid-rigging agreements 56
Greater transparency in the system of contract management in public procurement 59
References 66

4 Business integrity and competition among public procurement suppliers in Quebec 69

Communicating with the private sector and strengthening business integrity 70
Using enhanced controls on the integrity of companies wishing to enter into contracts with public and municipal bodies 75
Reconciling regulatory constraints, standards and certifications with a high level of competition in public procurement 80
Adapting bidding deadlines to the reality of the markets to increase participation in calls for tenders 87
References 92
Notes 94

5 The importance of contract performance in detecting, preventing and managing the risks of fraud and bribery in Quebec 95
Stakeholder accountability for transparent and efficient management of contract performance 96
Defining strategic contractual relationships with the private sector: a means of fighting corruption 103
References 110
Note 112

FIGURES

Figure 1.1. Number of countries that have developed mechanisms to systematise integrity policies in ministries among 34 OECD member or partner countries 17
Figure 2.1. Public Investment Cycle 34
Figure 2.2. Existence of a short list of all infrastructure projects to be implemented in the medium-term in OECD countries 38
Figure 2.3. Percentage of procedures used by public bodies above the thresholds for the period 2016-17 and 2015-16 40
Figure 3.1. Percentage of procedures used by public bodies below the thresholds for the period 2016-17 and 2015-16 51
Figure 3.2. Percentage of procedures used by public bodies above the thresholds for the period 2016-17 and 2015-16 53
Figure 3.3. Functionalities of e-procurement systems in OECD countries 63
Figure 4.1. Market analysis process of the Italian central purchasing body, Consip SpA 74
Figure 5.1. Number of new RENA registrations per year 97
Figure 5.2. Approach to public procurement 100
Figure 5.3. Loss of influence of procurement officials in public works contracts 104

TABLES

Table 1.1. Number of public and municipal organisations in Quebec 16
Table 1.2. Main actors in the oversight of public procurement in Quebec 30
Table 4.1. Examples of objectives, monitoring measures and impact indicators that could be established by the AMP 79
Table 4.2. Average period for submission of bids (in number of days) for CFTs 88
Table 5.1. Volume of purchases (in number and value) over the last 3 financial years 98

Abbreviations and acronyms

ACPB	Act respecting contracting by public bodies
AMF	Autorité des marchés financier (Financial Market Authority)
AMP	Autorité des marchés publics (Public Procurement Authority)
ANAC	*Autorità Nazzionale Anticorruzione* (National Anti-Corruption Agency)
APS	American Purchasing Society
BCP	Bureau du commissaire aux plaintes (Office of the Complaints Commissioner)
BIG	Bureau de l'inspecteur général de la ville de Montréal (Office of the Inspector General of the City of Montréal)
BIOS	*Bureau Integriteitsbevordering Openbare Sector* (National Ethics Office)
BNQ	Bureau de normalisation du Québec (Quebec Standardization Bureau)
BPME	Bureau des petites et moyennes entreprises (Office of Small and Medium-sized Enterprises)
BRIAS	Bid-Rigging Indicator Analysis System
CA	Contracting Authority
CCAF	Comité d'audit de l'administration fédérale (Audit Committee of the Federal Administration)
CETA	Canada-European Union Comprehensive Economic and Trade Agreement
CFT	Call for Tenders
CFTA	Canadian Free Trade Agreement
CMP	Contract Management Policy
CMQ	Commission municipale du Québec (Quebec Municipal Commission)
COAG	Council of Australian Governments
CSPQ	Centre de services partagés du Québec (Shared Services Centre of Quebec)
DGT	Direction générale territoriale (Territorial General Directorate)
EU	European Union
FQM	Fédération québécoise des municipalités (Quebec Federation of Municipalities)

FRVI	Forum des responsables de la vérification interne (Forum of Internal Audit Leaders)
GTCF	*Grupo de Trabajo sobre la Coordinación para la Fiscalización* (Working Group on Audit Coordination)
IEC	Independent Experts Committee
IIA	Institute of Internal Auditors
IMSS	*Instituto Mexicano de Seguro Social* (Social Security Institute of Mexico)
ISO	International Organisation for Standardisation
ITT	Invitation To Tender
LAMP	Loi sur l'Autorité des marchés publics (Act respecting the Autorité des marchés publics)
LCC	Life Cycle Cost
LCLCC	Anti-Corruption Act
LCV	Cities and Towns Act
MAMH	Ministry of Municipal Affairs and Housing
MIT	*Ministero delle Infrastrutture e dei Trasporti* (Ministry of Infrastructure and Transport)
MTESS	Ministry of Labour, Employment and Social Solidarity
MTQ	Quebec Ministry of Transportation
NHS	National Health System
NPO	Non-profit organisation
OECD	Organisation for Economic Cooperation and Development
OFPP	Office of Federal Procurement Policy
OGPR	Office of Public Procurement Review
OQTCA	Ontario-Quebec Trade and Cooperation Agreement
PGAGL	Programme gouvernemental d'apprentissage du gestionnaire-leader (Government Manager-Leader Apprenticeship Programme)
PIMAC	Public and Private Infrastructure Investment Management Center
PSDPA	Public Servants Disclosure Protection Act
PSPC	Public Services and Procurement Canada
QAG	Quebec Auditor General
RAMQ	Régie de l'assurance maladie du Québec (Quebec Health Insurance Board)
RARC	Responsable de l'application des règles contractuelles (Office responsible for enforcing contractual rules)
RCAOP	Règlement sur certains contrats d'approvisionnement des organismes publics (Regulation respecting certain supply contracts of public bodies)
RCM	Regional County Municipality

RCOPTI	Règlement sur les contrats des organismes publics en matière de technologies de l'information (Regulation respecting contracts of public bodies in the field of information technology)
RENA	Registre des entreprises non admissibles aux contrats publics (Register of companies ineligible for government contracts)
SAB	Standards Assessment Body
SAI	Supreme Audit Institutions
SAM	System for Award Management
SAP	Sourcing Activities Plan
SCC	Standards Council of Canada
SEAO	Système électronique d'appel d'offres (Electronic Tendering System)
SIS	Special Investigation Service
SQI	Société québécoise des infrastructures (Quebec Infrastructure Society)
TBS	Treasury Board Secretariat
UGAP	Union des groupements d'achats publics (Centralised public purchasing organisation)
UMQ	Union des municipalités du Québec (Union of Quebec Municipalities)
UPAC	Unité permanente anticorruption (Permanent Anti-Corruption Unit)

Executive summary

The fight against corruption in public procurement, a particularly vulnerable sector, requires a framework and actors capable of responding to a multitude of risks affecting the entire public procurement cycle. Quebec has taken an ambitious step in response to the recommendations of the Charbonneau Commission. Optimal application of these measures could have a decisive impact on public confidence in its governmental institutions and in their management of public funds. In order to complement recent reforms and strengthen the efforts undertaken, Quebec could define a comprehensive and strategic approach that would enable it to anticipate the risk of corruption affecting the conduct of public procurement.

Main findings

Quebec has invested undeniable efforts to prevent corruption in public procurement, and these efforts would benefit from being implemented through an integrated approach in a decentralised context. Several agencies are empowered to exercise extensive oversight powers over all public procurement in Quebec, but a proactive co-ordination strategy could increase the efficiency of these measures. Quebec has already laid the foundations for this strategy by developing a risk management methodology for the conduct of public procurement aligned with international best practices.

Although the work of the Independent Experts Committee (IEC) on increasing the transparency of the Ministry of Transportation's (MTQ) planning process was positively received, its mandate could be formalised. The decentralised planning processes of public and municipal agencies could be better supervised and co-ordinated in order to be integrated into a strategic approach.

The integrity of public procurement requires adequate procurement methods and transparency. Quebec has undertaken major efforts in this regard, but could strengthen consistency and coherence in the use of exceptions to calls for tenders (CFT). Moreover, despite the possibility of using several award criteria, the lowest price is still the one most frequently used. Transparency, particularly for the upstream phase and the performance of contracts, could be improved by adding features to the Quebec Electronic Tendering System (Le système électronique d'appel d'offres du gouvernement du Québec, SEAO).

Increased competition is an important element in the fight against corruption. Thus, measures governing relations between contracting authorities and the private sector or imposing regulatory requirements and controls on bidders must not be to the detriment of competition. In addition, Quebec could better adapt the bidding timelines to the complexity of the contracts, since approximately one-third of CFTs are subject to *addenda* delaying the closing of bids.

The contract performance phase in procurement is particularly vulnerable to integrity risks in public procurement. The majority of the economic consequences of corruption are concentrated at this stage of the public procurement cycle. Thus, the Government of Quebec has developed an extensive legislative and institutional arsenal that makes it possible to subject the performance of contracts to increased oversight. From the powers entrusted to the Autorité des marchés publics (AMP) to the control measures prior to the awarding of public contracts, all these initiatives seek to insulate public procurement from acts of corruption in the performance of public contracts.

Main recommendations

Quebec can strengthen the co-ordination of its integrity actions by establishing more restrictive benchmarks for all public bodies, as well as increased support and evaluation measures for the municipal environment, all while maintaining decentralisation of enforcement responsibilities. Supervisory bodies with potentially overlapping mandates could co-ordinate their supervision activities based on a risk analysis and take account of the comparative advantages of each institution. By considering their unique expertise and perspective, supervisory bodies could significantly contribute to defining the strategic approach, support and knowledge sharing on integrity in public procurement and thus play a significant preventive role.

Quebec could build on the recent successes of the IEC by formalising it in a law or directive and considering extending its activities to all major infrastructure projects. The process of needs identification could also be solidified and harmonised in public and municipal agencies.

The Government of Quebec could further promote the use of competitive procedures and review the system of exceptions to CFTs, while strengthening their control. Multiple award criteria and "life cycle cost" could be more widely used to improve competition. The government would benefit from increased transparency in the upstream phase (procurement plans) and the contract performance phase. Given the key role of the SEAO in strengthening integrity, the government could continue its digitisation efforts by incorporating additional functionalities and setting clear deadlines for mandatory electronic submission of bids.

The operationalisation of the contract authorisation regime could be improved by defining measurable objectives in advance in order to assess its performance and its impact on the conduct of public procurement, and by adapting its scope according to the risks inherent in each tender. The Government of Quebec would benefit from taking greater account of the impact of regulatory requirements on competition and on the access of Canadian suppliers outside Quebec in its public procurement.

Given the importance of government contracts in Quebec in terms of number and value, an effective strategy to combat corruption at the contract performance stage requires the mobilisation of all stakeholders to achieve this objective. In this way, audit institutions could prioritise their controls on the basis of objective risk indicators and focus their efforts on the most vulnerable contracts. Additionally, the Government of Quebec could strengthen and harmonise the roles of those directly involved in the performance of public procurement contracts. Indeed, the latter, whether they are public, such as the officer responsible for enforcing contractual rules (RARC), or private, such as site auditors, have varying responsibilities and a degree of accountability depending on the contract and the contracting authority. Stronger and wider harmonisation of their responsibilities would allow the development of a contractual management framework that is resilient to corruption risks.

1 Strengthening Integrity in Public procurement in Quebec

This chapter analyses the institutional and regulatory frameworks put in place by Quebec to adequately address the risks of corruption in public procurement. First, this chapter analyses the institutional framework of public and municipal agencies to ensure consistent enforcement of integrity standards in public procurement and a capacity-building approach. The chapter then looks in more detail at the enforcement of the standards from: i) monitoring and evaluation of their implementation, in a context of strong decentralisation; and ii) the development of training adapted to the needs of public procurement specialists at different management levels. Finally, the chapter concludes with an analysis of the framework for managing corruption risk and control in public procurement at the governmental and municipal levels.

To achieve high standards of integrity and performance in public procurement, it is essential that the relevant institutions co-ordinate effectively and with well-defined responsibilities, especially in contexts characterised by strong decentralisation. Public institutions must also implement guidance and monitoring measures, as well as reliable indicators that will enable them to effectively monitor the implementation of relevant policies and standards. These indicators must be developed and prioritised according to a strategic approach based on risk and the achievement of predefined institutional objectives.

Developing an integrated institutional framework to implement a coherent approach to integrity across government and municipalities

The Government of Quebec has made significant progress in recent years towards establishing an institutional framework of integrity in public procurement processes applicable to public and municipal organisations. Thus, two distinct institutional frameworks apply in the Quebec public sector: one governing contracts of government ministries and agencies (public bodies) and the other governing contracts of municipal bodies (Table 1.1). When it comes to integrity and transparency, these two regulatory frameworks are, except for a few details, very similar. However, the institutional framework of the Quebec government could adopt a more co-ordinated approach to the implementation of integrity standards in public and municipal bodies, which currently operate in a highly decentralised context.

Table 1.1. Number of public and municipal organisations in Quebec

Regulatory frameworks	Lead Ministry	Targeted Networks	Number
Public Bodies	Treasury Board Secretariat (TBS)	Ministries and Agencies Education Network Health and Social Services Network State-owned enterprises	315
Municipal Bodies	Ministry of Municipal Affairs and Housing (MAMH)	Municipalities Municipal Bodies	± 1 430

Source: Answers to the OECD questionnaire provided by the Government of Quebec.

Developing binding standards for the establishment of integrity infrastructures within public bodies

In Quebec, each public body is ultimately responsible for setting up institutional frameworks for integrity. However, within public organisations, there are more binding standards specifically applicable to the public procurement context than to integrity in general.

Integrating the institutional framework for public procurement into the general integrity framework for public bodies

Greater co-ordination between institutional frameworks for public procurement and integrity in the civil service could strengthen integrity standards applicable to the specific context of public procurement. Article 21.0.1 of the Act respecting contracting by public bodies (ACPB) requires each public body to designate an officer responsible for enforcing contractual rules (RARC) to ensure co-ordination between public procurement branches and agency leaders. The RARC's broad mandate allows him or her to play a key role in strengthening the compliance of public procurement processes with applicable rules. The RARC is responsible for ensuring compliance with contracting activities and for providing assurance to the head of the contracting authority (who is ultimately accountable) that the ACPB and other standards for the conduct of public procurement are respected. He or she is also responsible for ensuring that measures are in place within the organisation to ensure the integrity of internal processes and the quality of personnel performing contracting activities.

As such, the RARC is responsible for determining the specific controls and procedures to ensure compliance with the ACPB, while respecting the general guidelines suggested by the Directive regarding Managing Supplies, Service and Construction Contracts of Public Bodies and the Directive regarding Managing the Risk of Corruption and Collusion in Contract Management Processes. This approach, where a central agency is responsible for ensuring the development of a co-ordinated approach to integrity in the civil service, while promoting "proximity management" regarding the development and enforcement of rules by each public body, is aligned with best practice in OECD member countries.

Indeed, a large number of countries provide for a combination of regulatory requirements and guidance formulated by central government, with specialised units in sectoral ministries to formalise integrity policies (Figure 1.1).

Figure 1.1. Number of countries that have developed mechanisms to systematise integrity policies in ministries among 34 OECD member or partner countries

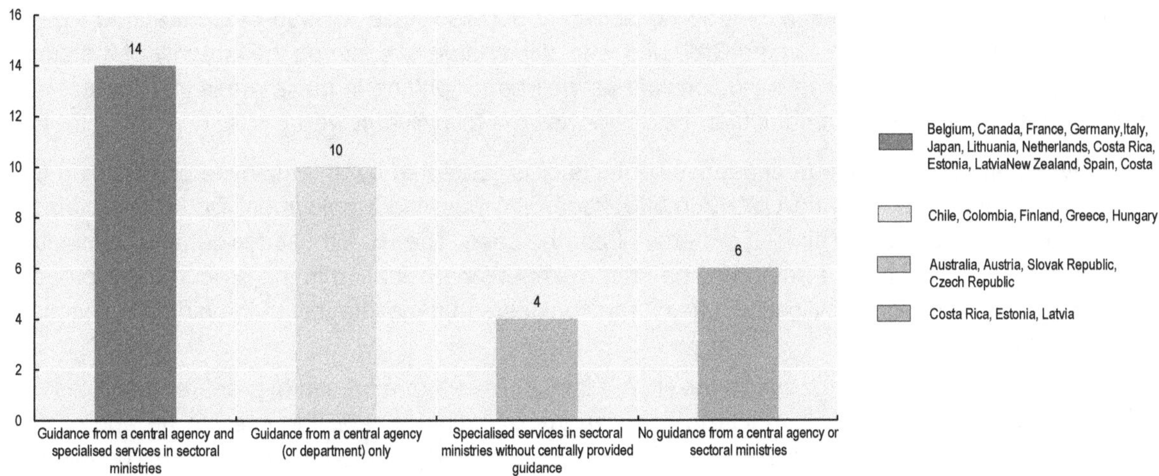

Source: OECD (2016), Public Sector Integrity Survey, OECD, Paris.

However, most of the institutional arrangements and mechanisms to ensure integrity in public procurement in OECD member countries are embedded in some way in the overall government integrity framework. For example, the institutional framework in the United States is similar to that of Quebec, especially regarding the appointment of the RARC as the procurement integrity officer (Box 1.1). Nevertheless, an important distinction is that a federal agency or department must appoint a Procurement Ethics Officer, who works closely with the Senior Procurement Executives and the Chief Acquisition Officers. Other OECD countries, such as Germany, New Zealand, and Norway, delegate responsibilities for ensuring integrity in public procurement to designated resources for general integrity issues to ensure a co-ordinated and consistent approach.

Box 1.1. Integrity of Public Procurement in United-States Government Agencies

In the United States, the majority of federal government contracts are governed by the Federal Acquisition Regulation system, which consists of all laws, rules and regulations applicable to federal public procurement.

Each federal agency or department is required to appoint a Designated Agency Ethics Official (DAEO) to co-ordinate an ethics programme and to respond to any requests for integrity advice from high-ranking procurement officials.

Government agencies are also required to appoint a Senior Procurement Executive (SPE) and sixteen of them[1] are required to appoint a Chief Acquisition Officer (CAO). Both are responsible for co-ordinating the agency's contracting system and ensuring the proper enforcement of existing laws and internal processes. The functions of the CAO include overseeing the procurement process, co-ordinating the evaluation of contractors' performance, advising the leader of the agency, and providing clear guidance on the responsibilities of procurement officers, while the SPE is responsible for the day-to-day management of the procurement process.

Within each federal agency, each contracting activity must also have a Head of Contracting Activity (HCA) who reports to the SPE and the CAO and who is in charge of ensuring the integrity of the public procurement for which he or she is responsible as well as for putting in place measures to deal with potential conflicts of interest. In particular, he or she has the following powers:

- When an official of a federal agency contacts or is contacted by an employee of a bidding firm (for a contract exceeding USD 250 000) regarding possible employment for that official, the official must disqualify himself or herself from the case. The HCA must decide, after consulting the Ethics Officer, to re-authorise the staff member's participation in the procurement process or to extend the disqualification if he or she considers that the integrity of the bidding process is threatened.
- Contracting officers must inform the HCA if they believe that a breach of procurement rules has occurred. The HCA may decide to open an investigation or refer the case to an appropriate investigative body. In all cases, he or she advises the staff member on the steps to be taken; if the contract has not yet been awarded, he or she may, for example, advise cancelling the tendering procedure or disqualifying a bidder.

Notes: 1. Departments of Agriculture, Commerce, Education, Energy, Health and Human Services, Homeland security, Housing and Urban Development, the Interior, Labor State, Transportation, Treasury, Veterans Affairs, Environmental Protection Agency, National Aeronautics and Space Administration, General Services Administration (GSA).

Source: Federal Acquisition Regulation (3.104 Procurement Integrity); (U.S. Office of government Ethics, 2007[11]), *Ethics & Procurement Integrity*, https://www.oge.gov/web/oge.nsf/Education%20Resources%20for%20Ethics%20Officials/7D9F7E91B7DF89BE85257FB6003E2917/$FILE/bkprocurementintegrity_07.pdf?open.

In Quebec, there are no requirements for the co-ordination of the RARC with the general institutional framework applicable to integrity in public bodies. Some stakeholders also report that there is little co-ordination in practice between RARCs and ethics officers within public bodies.

At the central institution level, the governmental co-ordination in ethics of the Treasury Board Secretariat (TBS) does not appear to be formally involved in integrity management in public procurement processes either. For example, the governmental co-ordination in ethics is not involved in the application of the Directive regarding Managing Supplies, Service and Construction Contracts of Public Bodies, even though it deals with the management of conflicts of interest and communications of influence in contracts.

Moreover, the governmental co-ordination in ethics does not appear to have contributed to the Treasury Board Secretariat's Analysis Report on Internal Guidelines, which sets out best practices for the implementation of guidelines for contract management, including the management of conflicts of interest.

Therefore, to ensure a holistic and co-ordinated approach to integrity in public contracting that is integrated into the overall integrity framework, TBS may wish to consider increased collaboration between ethics respondents and RARCs to, for example, effectively guide RARCs in the implementation of the Directive regarding Managing Supplies, Service and Construction Contracts of Public Bodies, especially with respect to conflicts of interest and lobbying.

Providing support to municipalities and municipal officials in matters of integrity and public procurement

The Ministry of Municipal Affairs and Housing (MAMH) has jurisdiction to oversee municipal affairs under the Cities and Towns Act and the Municipal Code, including public procurement and integrity issues. There is no systemic approach to strengthening integrity in public procurement in municipalities of comparable size, but this may be partly explained by the desire to respect the autonomy of elected municipal officials.

Providing guidance tailored to the needs of municipalities to strengthen integrity in public procurement

The MAMH has implemented a large number of reforms to strengthen public integrity standards in municipalities since the emergence of corruption cases leading up to the Charbonneau Commission, and these reforms represent significant progress. In addition, the establishment of the Public Procurement Authority (AMP), with its audit and oversight powers, further strengthens the integrity framework for public procurement. All organisations under municipal control (e.g., NPOs) are now subject to the rules for awarding municipal contracts, which responds to another recommendation of the Charbonneau Commission.

As a result of legislative reforms in 2010 and 2011, municipal agencies are now required to adopt a Contract Management Policy (CMP), to make it available on the Internet and forward it to the relevant ministry. The MAMH follows up on the adoption of CMPs (99.3% of municipal agencies have complied with their obligation), but there is no follow-up on their completeness and the effectiveness of their implementation.

The MAMH has also recently made legislative amendments, through draft act 155, to make the disclosure arrangements set out in the *Act to facilitate the disclosure of wrongdoings relating to public bodies* applicable to municipal agencies.

In addition, and as recommended by the Charbonneau Commission, the MAMH has set up a centre of expertise in municipal contract management to assist municipalities in the conduct of their public procurement, but the implementation of this process is still in the preliminary stages. This centre of expertise covers certain subjects related to integrity, particularly at the stage of the identification of needs and the contract award process. This centre of expertise is in addition to two other similar centres created within the SQI (contract management in the construction sector) and the CSPQ (contract management in the information technology sector).

Other jurisdictions have also put in place similar mechanisms to consolidate technical expertise in public procurement within the same institution responsible for providing technical support to other public institutions that are part of a decentralised system. For example, New Zealand has consolidated public procurement expertise in the construction sector in the Infrastructure New Zealand agency. Public bodies retain control over the organisation of public procurement, but may request the necessary support from Infrastructure New Zealand. The State of New South Wales in Australia has done the same with Infrastructure NSW, as has British Columbia with Partnerships BC and Scotland with the Scottish Futures

Trust. All of these jurisdictions have realised the significant benefits of consolidating expertise in an entity that is tailored to its mandate.

According to the work plan of the centre of expertise on contract management at the municipal level, many of the needs identified that may impact on the integrity of processes throughout the procurement cycle are related to capacity building for municipalities. Several of the actions proposed to remedy these problems consist of publishing more information or standard tender clauses on the MAMH website, or through briefings intended for municipalities (e.g. muni-express). While sharing technical information can be useful in strengthening public procurement processes, even more guidance can be provided to elected officials and municipal officers through personalised advice tailored to specific situations, as the above-mentioned bodies do in the construction sector.

The mere provision of technical information to elected representatives or municipal officers through ad hoc publications may not be sufficient to apply the relevant standards to specific cases and thus increases the vulnerability of processes to potential wrongdoing, such as the exercise of undue influence. The centre of expertise's action plan on contract monitoring already provides for the financing of technical staff for specific stages of the public procurement cycle. Similarly, the MAMH could consider funding the resources committed by municipal associations (the Fédération québécoise des municipalités (FQM) and the Union des municipalités du Québec (UMQ)) to guide municipalities on an ongoing basis so that they avoid pitfalls that could compromise the integrity of all stages of the public procurement cycle. In addition, the MAMH could also consider whether the current training format meets the needs of public procurement officials at municipal level, and consider the implementation of certification programmes and new training programmes for elected municipal officials and public procurement professionals, as discussed in the "Providing support to municipalities and municipal officials in matters of integrity and public procurement" section of this report, related to Quebec government public bodies.

Applying the powers of the AMP to strike the right balance between its oversight activities, capacity building, and contract efficiency

Given the nature and scope of the powers conferred on the AMP, it interacts on a regular basis with both public and municipal bodies. Its oversight mandate, as well as its powers to issue orders for public bodies and to make recommendations for municipal bodies, play a key role in strengthening integrity in the conduct of all public procurement in Quebec. However, given the advanced expertise that the AMP has at different levels of public procurement, it could also play an important role in increasing efficiency by preventing irregularities in procurement processes, as well as by strengthening technical expertise in public and municipal bodies.

Defining the AMP's powers of intervention to ensure that they contribute to greater efficiency in the conduct of public procurement

The inauguration of the AMP coincided with the extension of the mandate of the Unité permanente anticorruption (Permanent Anti-Corruption Unit-UPAC) to corruption cases no longer exclusively related to public contracts. The sharing of administrative and criminal powers between the AMP and UPAC is a positive development that will lead to increased resources and expertise for the oversight of public contract management, as well as the investigation and prosecution of corruption in the provincial and municipal civil service.

Nevertheless, the increase in the AMP's oversight powers over public contracts is cause for concern among some public and municipal bodies. Some stakeholders interviewed for this report mentioned that increased monitoring of public servants in small municipalities could significantly increase their workload by imposing a results-based performance on them, despite the limited means at their disposal. Other stakeholders are concerned that the extensive powers of the AMP could be unduly used to delay the award of public contracts due to minor errors in the applicable rules.

When drawing up its strategic plan required by article 18 of the Act respecting the Autorité des marchés publics (LAMP), the AMP must provide for means of intervention adapted to the consequences of the violations against the public interest. The Government of Quebec may also consult the AMP to strengthen its prevention and technical knowledge-sharing activities, since the AMP is well-positioned to provide an external perspective under its monitoring and recommendation powers under the LAMP.

Finally, the AMP could develop a communication strategy aimed at all public and municipal bodies that would reiterate its willingness to adopt a constructive approach in supporting the bodies subject to its oversight powers, in line with the spirit of the LAMP. Indeed, the LAMP is structured in such a way that public and municipal bodies have the opportunity to self-correct before the AMP is called upon to intervene, except in cases where amendments are made to the tender documents less than two days before the expiry of the deadline for receiving complaints. In order to be more predictable, the AMP could also clearly specify through its communication strategy when the powers to amend or cancel a public procurement contract will be applied.

Defining values and standards of integrity and applying them to specific contexts

In line with best practice in OECD countries, the TBS and the MAMH have developed centralised standards for integrity and technical competence specific to public procurement in public and municipal bodies. The implementation of these standards is highly decentralised as each deputy minister or head of the contracting authority is responsible for their enforcement at the public agency level, as well as each municipal council at the municipal level. In order to strengthen accountability with respect to the definition and enforcement of integrity and performance values for professionals working in the public procurement sector, the Government of Quebec could consider developing additional monitoring and evaluation measures for all public and municipal bodies, combined with training tailored to specific contexts.

Monitoring and evaluation of integrity standards in all public bodies

To establish common civil service integrity values, the government adopted the *Regulation respecting ethics and discipline in the civil service* in 2002, which sets out the general ethical duties of public servants. Concerning public procurement specifically, the Government requires public bodies to adopt guidelines in line with the *Directive regarding Managing Procurement, Service and Construction Contracts of Public Bodies*.

However, the implementation of the Regulation and the Directive is highly decentralised. It is up to the head of each contracting authority to define the parameters for implementation in each public body. This decentralisation has led to uneven results from one agency to another. Moreover, according to a list available on the TBS website, there are 55 public bodies that are not subject to the *Public Service Act* and, therefore, to the regulations.

Developing monitoring and evaluation measures to strengthen the enforcement of specific public procurement integrity standards

The *Directive Respecting the Management of Supply, Service and Construction Contracts of Public Bodies* provides both a comprehensive regulatory framework specific to the conduct of public procurement as well as a code of conduct. However, the responsibility for enforcing these rules is highly decentralised, so public bodies ultimately have the discretion to develop and implement innovative policies to enhance integrity in their public procurement processes.

Indeed, several public organisations have developed integrity mechanisms in response to the Directive, which requires the adoption of guidelines on several aspects related to the integrity of public procurement, including the management of conflicts of interest and lobbying (SCT, 2016[2]).

For example, some public bodies, in accordance with standard documents developed by the TBS, require potential contractors to disclose if any of their employees were formerly employed in a public body. This practice seeks to ensure compliance with applicable post-employment rules. In order to further formalise this mechanism, work is currently under way to incorporate the clauses included in standard documents into the regulations on ethics and professional conduct in the civil service, as well as into regulations on public contracts.

The report on the analysis of internal guidelines for public bodies also aimed to identify overall areas for improvement and best practices related to integrity in public procurement for all public bodies. However, the report does not intend to provide a detailed analysis of all public bodies through comparing their performance. There is therefore no systematic monitoring and evaluation of the implementation of the guidelines.

There are several ways to increase the accountability of public bodies for the implementation of guidelines, policies, or other tools for integrity in public procurement in a decentralised framework. First, an obligation to implement centrally issued directives could be imposed in a law or regulation. Further, in order to follow up on the efforts made by public bodies, the law or regulation may require the head of the contracting authority to report annually on efforts to ensure effective implementation of the guidelines. For example, the Government of Canada requires, through the *Public Servants Disclosure Protection Act,* that the chief executives of ministries and agencies ensure the implementation of the Values and Ethics Code for the Public Sector, the Policy on Conflict of Interest and Post-Employment, their organisational code of conduct, and their whistleblowing procedures. Some governments also have measures for evaluating the implementation of integrity policies (Box 1.2). Others such as Austria, Costa Rica, the Netherlands, and the United Kingdom have also adapted audit methodologies to assess the implementation of different integrity policies in public bodies (EUROSAI, 2017[3]).

Box 1.2. Dissemination of integrity standards throughout the civil service in the Netherlands

In the Netherlands, the Ministry of the Interior is responsible for the implementation of integrity standards throughout the public administration. The Ministry is supported in this task by the National Integrity Office *(Bureau Integriteitsbevordering Openbare Sector*, BIOS), which operates as a centre of knowledge and expertise and supports public bodies in the implementation of integrity policies.

In collaboration with the BIOS and several public sector organisations (Association of Local Governments, Union of Public Water Authorities, Association of Provincial Agencies), the Ministry of the Interior has launched an initiative to assess the implementation of integrity standards in the civil service, entitled "Integrity Monitor". The main objectives of this monitor are:

- informing Parliament about the assessment of the integrity policies of the Dutch administration as well as the actions taken by the Ministry of the Interior on the reported results
- commiting all decentralised government services to comply with established integrity regulations and raise awareness of ethical issues.

The first "monitor" launched in 2004 assessed the implementation of integrity policies among the four levels of public administration and identified a lack of their implementation.

Since 2006, regular integrity perception surveys have been included in the assessments, leading to the development of an integrated monitoring process in 2012, which included a check-list of integrity policies, an inventory of the number of disciplinary proceedings and a survey on the perception of integrity policies and integrity culture. A survey on the perception of political mandate holders was included for the first time in 2012.

In order to strengthen the effectiveness of policies, special attention was devoted to integrity, aggression and violence in 2016. In particular, it targeted key groups such as public office holders, secretaries-general, directors and officials of central government, provinces, municipalities and public water authorities. The results identified anti-corruption priorities and key elements of an effective integrity policy, such as commitment at the highest level of an organisation and leadership by example.

Source: Presentation by Ms Marja van der Werf at the OECD Senior Public Integrity Officers (SPIO) meeting (4 November 2016, Paris).

As such, the Government of Quebec could delegate authority to the TBS to monitor and evaluate the measures implemented in the application of policies developed by TBS on integrity in public procurement, as well as their adaptation to the specific context of public agencies. To ensure greater consistency across the public sector, this monitoring and evaluation power could extend to all public bodies, including those not regulated under the *Public Service Act*.

This TBS monitoring mechanism could also resemble the assessment currently being conducted by the TBS and UPAC of the risk management plans developed by public bodies under the Directive Respecting the Management of Corruption and Collusion Risks in Contract Management Processes. Indeed, unlike the Directive Respecting the Management of Supply, Service and Construction Contracts of Public Bodies, the obligation to develop risk management plans with accompanying monitoring mechanisms provided for in the Directive on risk management, ensures that public bodies are held to account for its implementation periodically.

Developing training courses tailored to the needs of public procurement professionals to maximise their impact

Relevant training on integrity in public procurement within public organisations is mainly prescriptive and conducted by the TBS and UPAC. According to the information collected from stakeholders, integrity training focuses on senior officials or department heads, rather than on public procurement professionals. The Quebec government could consider developing training that goes beyond the statutory aspects and is more focused on the practical needs of professionals. In line with best practice in OECD member countries, these training courses may also aim to enhance the role and functions of public procurement professionals.

Customising training activities based on employee feedback and impact assessments, and ensuring that they are available to all procurement professionals

The TBS pays special attention to RARCs, senior and middle managers, and selection committee secretaries of public bodies for integrity training. For example, executives receive ethics training as part of the Government Manager-Leader Apprenticeship Programme (PGAGL). The RARCs and Selection Committee Secretaries, meanwhile, hold discussion forums addressing different aspects of contract management, including issues of integrity and conflict of interest in contracts on an annual basis. During these meetings, RARCs are also invited to raise awareness of integrity and conflict of interest issues with the employees involved in contract management within their organisation. Finally, Selection Committee Secretaries must pass an exam specifically addressing the knowledge required to perform this strategic function. This test is administered by the TBS, which also provides pre-test training sessions.

Training for public procurement professionals is delivered through courses or conferences and, to a lesser extent, through webinars. The TBS promotes face-to-face training for all public procurement managers and employees to encourage dialogue and discussions of practical cases to promote learning. According to statistics compiled by the TBS, webinars are mainly used for rapid dissemination of technical or administrative information, such as completing a form or meeting administrative formalities, or to reach professionals who are physically distant from urban centres.

However, according to the perceptions of the stakeholders consulted for this report, the majority of training available to public procurement professionals is in the form of webinars, and these are not suitable for discussing the practical aspects of rule enforcement. Other stakeholders added that the training was aimed more at managers than at employees responsible for public procurement. Therefore, there appears to be a gap between the availability of face-to-face training in public procurement and perceptions of the availability of such training by professionals. The Government of Quebec could, therefore, take steps to ensure that such training is disseminated to all professionals in each public body. This recommendation does not aim to reduce the number of training courses for managers, as they are key actors in disseminating common values and technical knowledge in the public sector, particularly in decentralised environments. Rather, the main purpose of the recommendation is to ensure that training is available and tailored to each segment of public procurement professionals in the Quebec civil service.

The Government of Quebec could also ensure that it collects comments on the content of the training courses as well as statistics on the number and identity of participants. Together, this data could help to determine whether the training courses are reaching all public procurement professionals and meeting their needs. Finally, to complement traditional training, the Quebec government could implement mentoring, pairing or temporary rotation programmes between different public bodies to stimulate learning from other perspectives and promote the dissemination of best practices.

Co-ordinating the different centres of technical expertise to maximise the relevance of training activities on integrity in public procurement

Through the nature of its mandate and its oversight and control functions, the AMP is in a strategic position to assess the need for technical knowledge building in both public and municipal agencies. Using AMP's monitoring and recommendation powers with regard to training would make it possible to integrate considerations and practical cases experienced by the organisation during its interventions in order to supplement the more traditional regulatory content (Box 1.3). As one of the objectives of the creation of the AMP was to bring together highly qualified professionals with varied expertise in different aspects of public procurement, this organisation would be well-positioned to judge the relevance and effectiveness of the training delivered to public officials in the field of public procurement.

Box 1.3. Integrity training for public procurement officers in Germany

Germany has introduced systematic integrity training for public procurement officers.

Since 2001, participation in a corruption prevention workshop has been mandatory for new employees of the Federal Public Procurement Agency, a government agency that manages public procurement for 26 federal authorities, foundations and research institutes under the responsibility of the Federal Minister of the Interior. The training covers the risks associated with involvement in corruption, the strategies of corrupt actors, and the appropriate reactions when these situations occur, for example by encouraging staff to report them ("whistleblowing"). In 2005, the target group for this training was expanded to include not only an introductory session but also continued training for all staff. Since then, 6 to 7 workshops have been held each year, training approximately 70 new and existing employees per year.

This training is in addition to other key measures put in place by the Public Procurement Agency to promote integrity among its staff, including the support and advice of a Corruption Prevention Officer ("Corruption Prevention Contact Person") and staff rotation. The latter measure, which requires employee rotation after a period of five to eight years, in order to avoid prolonged contact with suppliers, improve motivation and make work more engaging. However, if staff cannot change posts because their knowledge and high level of specialisation are essential to the work of their unit, alternative measures such as intensified monitoring (oversight) are taken.

Source: Federal Procurement Agency of the Ministry of the Interior, Germany, http://www.bescha.bund.de/DE/Startseite/home_node.html.

By virtue of its monitoring and recommendation powers, the AMP could evaluate training activities conducted by the government and municipal associations (Fédération québécoise des municipalités, Union des municipalités du Québec), particularly through the newly created centres of expertise within the CSPQ, the SQI and the MAMH, and make recommendations to the Government of Quebec and the municipalities on improving training if necessary. AMP advice on technical training could potentially ensure consistency of information provided through training at the provincial and municipal levels.

Valuing the public procurement specialist profession

Finally, the information gathered from stakeholders reveals that the public procurement departments within government organisations suffer loss of expertise due to high turnover among public procurement professionals. These professionals have to adapt to frequent changes in rules and processes, high workloads and high expectations given the short time frames involved in conducting public procurement processes. Based on discussions with stakeholders, the importance of the role of public procurement professionals is not always well understood and promoted within the Quebec civil service.

In response to concerns expressed about the high turnover of public procurement specialists compared to, for example, inspection and audit, the Government of Quebec may consider developing and implementing a certification programme for public procurement professionals. The TBS already administers a similar programme for Selection Committee Secretaries, which could be used to extract best practices for training and testing the knowledge and skills of procurement specialists. A certification programme could help to enhance the role of procurement professionals, plan for succession to offset employee turnover, and better equip professionals to meet the high demands of the profession (Box 1.4).

Box 1.4. Implementation of skills certification mechanisms or strategies aimed at better valuing the profession of public contracting officers

Canada

The Acquired Services and Assets Sector Communities Management Office (ASAS CMO) co-ordinates a federal government certification programme for federal public servants who specialise in procurement and material management. Launched in 2006, this nationally and internationally recognised certification aims to provide better recognition of the profession and shared competencies in asset life cycle management, from needs assessment and planning through to acquisition and disposal. Two different types of qualifications - Certification as a Certified Federal Specialist in Procurement (Levels 1 and 2) or Certification as a Certified Federal Specialist in Materiel Management (Level 1) –are available.

United States

In the United States, the American Purchasing Society (APS) was the first organisation in the country to develop nationally recognised certification programmes for buyers and procurement professionals. The APS offers 3 certification programmes (Certified Professional Purchasing programs) respectively for professionals, managers and consultants respectively, working in a consulting or teaching capacity in the field of public procurement outside their main job.

United Kingdom

In the United Kingdom, the Public Procurement Service (PPS) has developed a strategy to train public procurement officers ("Build the Procurement Profession in Government"). The PPS does not provide certification but wants to build a "community" of public procurement officers characterised by key competencies that include: an understanding of business drivers such as profit, margins, ownership, cost models, acquisition costs and cost analysis over time, as well as knowledge of contract law.

Sources: Government of Canada, Certification Program for the Federal Public procurement and Materiel Management Communities, http://www.tpsgc-pwgsc.gc.ca/ongc-cgsb/certification/index-fra.html (accessed on 30 July 2018).
American Purchasing Society, *www.american-purchasing.com* (accessed 30 July 2018). Public procurement Service (2009), "Building the Procurement Profession in Government",
http://webarchive.nationalarchives.gov.uk/20101008013828/http://www.ogc.gov.uk/documents/GPS_Strategy.pdf
(accessed 30 July 2018).

Risk management and optimal controls to strengthen prevention and accountability

Maximising the performance of a risk management framework for all public bodies

Since 2016, the Government of Quebec has made significant efforts to develop and implement a risk management culture for the conduct of public procurement in a large number of public and municipal bodies. These efforts take into account the recommendations of the Quebec Auditor General (QAG) and the Anti-Corruption Commissioner on implementing plans to manage the risk of corruption and collusion in the contracting processes of all public bodies (Anti-corruption Commissioner, 2017[4]; VGQ, 2016[5]).

Using the information generated by the risk management framework in an optimal manner for contract management

Public bodies subject to the ACPB are required, under the *Directive regarding Managing the Risk of Corruption and Collusion in Contract Management Processes*, to adopt a risk management plan to strengthen the integrity of their contracting processes. The UPAC has developed a robust and effective tool to guide public bodies in the analysis and development of adequate responses to the risk of corruption, namely the *Guide d'élaboration d'un modèle de cadre organisationnel de gestion des risques de corruption et de collusion dans les processus de gestion contractuelle* (Guide to developing a model organisational framework for managing corruption and collusion risks in contract management processes - the Guide). The UPAC has also developed a toolbox to facilitate the implementation of the Directive which includes 45 standard risks in the management of public contracts. The UPAC's risk management approach is inspired by ISO 31000, ISO 37001 and the International Standards for the Professional Practice of Internal Auditing (IIA).

The UPAC also conducts several coaching and knowledge-sharing sessions in public bodies for the development of their risk management plans, and feedback from stakeholders has been positive. The development of risk management plans for public bodies that are more vulnerable to the risk of corruption have been prioritised, in line with best practice.

In order to maximise its usefulness and awareness potential, the UPAC and TBS could also provide guidance to public bodies to define precisely how the information generated by risk management plans on an ongoing basis will be used, beyond the strengthening of existing internal controls. Indeed, the development of a risk management plan should not be an end in itself; the information gathered should be used strategically. For example, it could be used to update and improve integrity training for public officials and to develop or better target awareness campaigns in public bodies.

Mitigating the risk of corruption or ethical abuses at the municipal level

The UPAC offers consulting services to municipalities and regional county municipalities (RCMs) in Quebec to help them assess the risks associated with corruption and collusion. The UPAC's mandate with respect to municipalities is derived from Article 3 of the Anti-Corruption Act (LCLCC), which includes all municipalities in its definition of 'public sector'. As for public bodies, the services offered by the UPAC to municipal agencies are mainly based on the *Guide to developing a model organisational framework for managing corruption and collusion risks in contract management processes*, the related toolkit, and training provided by the UPAC.

Supporting the development and implementation of risk management plans in public procurement in municipalities or RCMs

The adoption of a risk management plan by municipalities is not mandatory since municipalities are not subject to the *Directive regarding Managing the Risk of Corruption and Collusion in Contract Management Processes*. However, the methodology proposed by UPAC for all municipalities and RCMs in Quebec could apply to all municipalities, be tailored to the size and context of each one. The methodology has also been the subject of pilot projects conducted with the *Régie de l'assurance maladie du Québec* (RAMQ), the MTQ and Ville de Sorel-Tracy.

Although the MAMH reported a growing interest of municipalities in strengthening their management of corruption risk in public contracts, the UPAC's interventions revealed that international best practices in risk management and internal control (e.g. the best practices of the Institute of Internal Auditors (IIA)) are not part of the municipalities' culture. Neither the MAMH, nor the *Commission municipale du Québec* (CMQ), nor the AMP plan to provide guidance on managing the risk of corruption, fraud or collusion. Finally, the public organisations surveyed were very satisfied with the support services that UPAC had provided in developing their risk management plans.

Once the bulk of the work for the development and implementation of the first risk management plans for public bodies is accomplished, the Government of Quebec could specifically request that the UPAC support the development and implementation of these plans in municipalities or RCMs that are above a certain size or that are at particular risk of corruption and collusion. Support for municipalities by an anti-corruption agency at central government level has already been tried in some OECD countries, including Lithuania, where good results have been achieved (Box 1.5).

Box 1.5. The Special Investigation Service in Lithuania supports municipalities in dealing with the risk of corruption

In Lithuania, each regional entity or municipality is required to develop a comprehensive risk management strategy, which has to be validated by the Special Investigation Service (SIS). The SIS reviews each of the strategies, including risk assessment, and may make recommendations or conduct further analysis if an institution is vulnerable corruption risks within certain predetermined parameters. The review results in a report providing analyses and recommendations that the institutions reviewed must consider within six months.

Each year, the SIS conducts risk analyses in approximately 16 state or municipal institutions. One of the priorities for the SIS in the coming years is the development of training and guidance to strengthen the capacity of public entities and municipalities in the development and implementation of corruption risk management strategies.

Source: OECD (unpublished), *Lithuania's Accession to the OECD Report*.

A robust and independent internal audit function to contribute to the integrity of public procurement

Public procurement is a sector that is particularly vulnerable to the risk of corruption and collusion. The establishment of a robust and independent internal audit function should be at the forefront of any risk management and internal control strategy to prevent and detect corruption and collusion in public procurement.

Ensuring an adequate level of expertise and independence for the internal audit function in all public bodies

In the spring of 2016, the QAG published a study that shows a significant gap between several public bodies regarding the status of institutional arrangements for internal audit within the Quebec government. Indeed, there is no systemic approach to internal audit in the Quebec civil service, with the *Public Administration Act* stipulating the role of each deputy minister and agency leader in exercising controls related to results-based management.

Some mechanisms have been established to strengthen procurement surveillance. For example, the MTQ has set up a Contract Management Quality Assurance Directorate, whose functions include the analysis of contract documents before contracts are awarded and, in some cases, after the fact to verify various control mechanisms provided for in the ministry's directives and procedures.

In order to improve co-ordination and knowledge sharing among internal audit teams, the Government of Quebec has developed the *Guide de vérification du processus de gestion contract* (Audit Guide for the contract management process) (2014) and the Forum of Internal Audit Leaders (FRVI), which brings together the heads of internal audit working within the Quebec public administration. The Audit Guide proposes various approaches based on ISO 31000 and the IIA International Standards for conducting internal audits of contract management processes, including methodologies for planning internal audits. However, these initiatives alone have not been sufficient to ensure a particular level of expertise and consistency in control systems across public bodies (VGQ, 2016[6]).

Another issue relates to the independence of internal audit in government ministries, where more than 50% of the members of internal audit committees are from within the public body itself, which entails risks to the objectivity of audits. Finally, the QAG report concludes that many of the internal audit units have insufficient knowledge of risks and controls outside their ministries (VGQ, 2016[6]).

Conversely, entities subject to the *Act respecting the governance of state-owned enterprises* have several good internal audit practices in place. This would allow the government to draw on the means provided for in the Act to strengthen the requirements applicable to other public bodies, for example, considering the establishment of an audit committee with independent and appropriately qualified members for each public body. This committee would be responsible, among other things, for approving the annual internal audit plan, ensuring that internal control mechanisms are in place and that they are adequate and effective, and ensuring that a risk management process is in place. The *Act respecting the governance of state-owned enterprises* also requires the audit committee to notify the board of directors (the minister or head of the contracting authority in the case of a public body that does not have a board of directors) in writing if it identifies any operations or management practices that are not sound or that do not comply with the relevant internal laws, regulations or policies (VGQ, 2016[6]).

To ensure consistency in the implementation of good internal audit practices across the civil service, the Government of Quebec, through the TBS or another body, could impose internal auditing rules and standards including some of the measures provided for in the *Act respecting the governance of state-owned enterprises*. These guidelines could provide for the establishment of an audit committee with independent members to ensure the oversight and quality of internal audit activities conducted by audit management in public bodies. The norms and standards could also provide for capacity-building activities administered by the TBS for all public bodies to ensure an adequate level of skills. In addition, the TBS could be authorised to issue recommendations to public bodies to strengthen their internal audit capacity, including performance appraisals. Finally, these rules and standards could be enshrined in a law or directive to make them mandatory.

Adopting a proactive and balanced approach to the management of public procurement oversight activities by external bodies

Several external bodies have extensive oversight powers regarding the conduct of public procurement in Quebec. In some cases, these bodies have complementary powers of prevention and inspection or investigation. Some oversight bodies co-ordinate their activities in this way to increase their effectiveness and avoid heavy caseloads.

One of the strengths of Quebec's system for fighting corruption in the conduct of public procurement is the delegation of extensive oversight powers to several bodies, some of which do not report directly to the executive branch. Their mandate is to oversee the enforcement of various regulatory frameworks for the management of public contracts (Table 1.2).

Table 1.2. Main actors in the oversight of public procurement in Quebec

	Main responsibilities in the area of public procurement management
Autorité des marchés publics Public Procurement Authority	• Conducts audits on a contracting process following a complaint, or on its own initiative • Conducts administrative investigations into the contractual management of public bodies
Anti-Corruption Commissioner	• Reviews whistleblowing and co-ordinates investigations of collusion and corruption at provincial and municipal levels • Makes recommendations and works on prevention/education in the fight against corruption
Auditor General	• Conducts administrative audits and investigations relating to the management of public funds by public bodies
Commission municipale du Québec Quebec Municipal Commission	• Conducts public inquiries into a municipality's financial administration • Acts as mediator and arbitrator in municipal disputes
Inspecteur général de la ville de Montréal Inspector General of the City of Montreal	• Oversees the City of Montréal's contracting process • Conducts audits and investigations of the City of Montréal contracts and related legal persons
Treasury Board Secretariat	• Ensures the proper administration of public procurement at the level of public bodies • Conducts audits as a complement to its normative role (continuous improvement of contracting processes) • Provides training on the regulatory framework
Ministry of Municipal Affairs and Housing	• Ensures the proper administration of public procurement at the municipal level • Conducts audits relating to contract management, particularly in response to a complaint

Source: Response of the Government of Quebec to the OECD Questionnaire, 2018.

Formalising information-sharing to facilitate the planning of oversight and investigation activities among oversight agencies

As a result of the establishment of the AMP and the reforms brought about by draft act 155 regarding independent auditing in municipalities, there is now a large number of different actors responsible for external audits of public and municipal bodies in terms of compliance and resource optimisation. Effective co-ordination can enable them to fulfil their oversight mandate more effectively, which is all the more important considering that for all public and municipal agencies combined, there were more than 30 000 government contracts in 2016-17, worth more than USD 16 billion.

The LAMP stipulates that the AMP may share information brought to its attention with the Inspector General of the City of Montreal, the Ombudsman, the Anti-Corruption Commissioner, the TBS and the MAMH, depending on the nature of the information. According to article 71 of the LAMP, these institutions will have to sign an agreement specifically for this purpose. Additionally, several stakeholders indicated in interviews that they would immediately forward any information relevant to the mandate of another oversight institution that came to their attention.

However, it could be beneficial to formalise not only *a posteriori* information sharing, but also to co-ordinate upstream oversight activities for greater efficiency. Indeed, although *a posteriori* information sharing is essential to detecting and reacting to irregularities or acts of corruption in the conduct of public procurement, co-ordinating the planning of upstream oversight activities in order to avoid duplication and to ensure that the main risk areas are subject to an appropriate level of controls is also crucial.

Thus, in order to adopt a co-ordinated and proactive approach, the TBS and the internal audit bodies of government agencies could consider co-ordinating, to some extent, the planning of their oversight activities to avoid duplication and to enhance, to the extent possible, their coherence and effectiveness. The oversight bodies provided for in article 71 of the LAMP could also ensure that the exchange of information under the LAMP goes in both directions - between the AMP on the one hand; and the UPAC, the Office of the Inspector General of Ville de Montréal (BIG), the Quebec Ombudsman, the TBS and the MAMH on the other. Quebec law could also provide for an agreement to formalise information sharing and avoid overlap in relation to oversight activities at the municipal level, for example between the MAMH, municipal auditors, CMQ, the UPAC and the AMP.

Finally, the information gathered for this report indicated that the QAG and government oversight bodies co-ordinate those aspects of their mandates that overlap. As such, the Government of Quebec, in partnership with the QAG, could explore the possibility of formalising their collaboration, drawing in particular on Mexico's National Audit System Co-ordinating Committee, which is responsible for co-ordinating the oversight activities of external and internal audit institutions at federal, state and municipal levels, despite the autonomy of these institutions under the Mexican Constitution.

Action plan

An integrated institutional framework

- Integrating the institutional framework for public procurement into the general integrity framework for public bodies
- Providing guidance tailored to the needs of municipalities to strengthen integrity in public procurement
- Defining the AMP's powers of intervention to ensure that they contribute to greater efficiency in the conduct of public procurement

The definition of common values

- Developing monitoring and evaluation measures to enforce the implementation of integrity standards specific to public procurement
- Customising training activities based on employee feedback and impact assessments, and ensuring that they are available to all procurement professionals
- Co-ordinating the different centres of technical expertise to maximise the relevance of training activities on integrity in public procurement
- Valuing the profession of public procurement specialist

Optimal risk management and controls

- Using the information generated by the risk management framework in an optimal manner for contract management
- Supporting the development and implementation of risk management plans in public procurement in municipalities or RCMs
- Ensuring an adequate level of expertise and independence for the internal audit function in all public bodies
- Formalising information-sharing to facilitate the planning of oversight and investigation activities among oversight agencies

References

Anti-corruption Commissioner (2017), *Annexe 11 : Cadre organisationnel de gestion des risques en matière de corruption et de collusion dans les processus de gestion contractuelle*, Politique sur les activités d'approvisionnement et la gestion des contrats, https://www.sf.ulaval.ca/regles-et-politiques/politique-sur-les-activites-dapprovisionnement-et-la-gestion-des-contrats/annexe-11 (accessed on 13 May 2020). [4]

EUROSAI (2017), *Guideline for Audit of Ethics in Public Sector Organisations*, https://www.sayistay.gov.tr/en/Upload/files/Ethics/Guidelines%20to%20audit%20ethics.pdf. [3]

SCT (2016), *Rapport d'analyse du Secrétariat du Conseil du trésor concernant les lignes internes de conduite*, Gouvernement du Québec, http://numerique.banq.qc.ca/patrimoine/details/52327/3195764. [2]

U.S. Office of government Ethics (2007), *Ethics & Procurement Integrity*, https://www.oge.gov/web/oge.nsf/Education%20Resources%20for%20Ethics%20Officials/7D9F7E91B7DF89BE85257FB6003E2917/. [1]

VGQ (2016), *Contrats d'achats regroupés en technologies de l'information*, Rapport du Vérificateur général du Québec, https://www.vgq.qc.ca/Fichiers/Publications/rapport-annuel/2016-2017-VOR-Printemps/fr_Rapport2016-2017-VOR-Chap02.pdf. [5]

VGQ (2016), *Portrait de la vérification interne au gouvernement du Québec*, Rapport du Vérificateur général du Québec, http://vgq.qc.ca/fr/fr_publications/fr_rapport-annuel/fr_2016-2017-VOR-Printemps/fr_Rapport2016-2017-VOR-Chap08.pdf. [6]

2 A strategic definition of the needs of public actors in Quebec

This chapter analyses the means put in place to depoliticise the Government of Quebec's infrastructure project planning. These measures aim to improve the transparency and accountability of public authorities at the identification of needs and public procurement planning stage for major infrastructure projects. Focusing primarily on the activities of the IEC, this chapter also looks more generally at overall procurement planning within government organisations.

In Quebec, as elsewhere, measures to increase transparency and accountability in the conduct of public procurement focus on the organisation and management phase of the call for tenders. However, the identification of needs and planning stage of public procurement are also highly vulnerable to undue influence and corruption. The identification of needs stage is particularly vulnerable in large infrastructure projects, especially because of the degree of government discretion in investment decisions, the size of the amounts involved, the technical complexity of the projects and the multi-stage nature of the investment cycle. According to the OECD's Foreign Bribery Report (OECD, 2014[1]), almost 60% of bribery cases that occur abroad take place in sectors closely related to infrastructure (mining, construction, transport and business, information and communication).

Political influence, particularly at the stages of identification of needs and project planning, can lead to waste and the creation of "white elephants" (i.e. infrastructure that does not meet needs and whose costs are not justified by its usefulness). Thus, governments should ensure that controls exist throughout the entire public investment policy cycle, not just at the stages associated with the tendering phase (Figure 2.1). Several countries have adopted measures to reduce the risk of politicisation in each of these phases and thus avoid infrastructure projects being captured for the benefit of inefficient economic actors or vested interests.

Figure 2.1. Public Investment Cycle

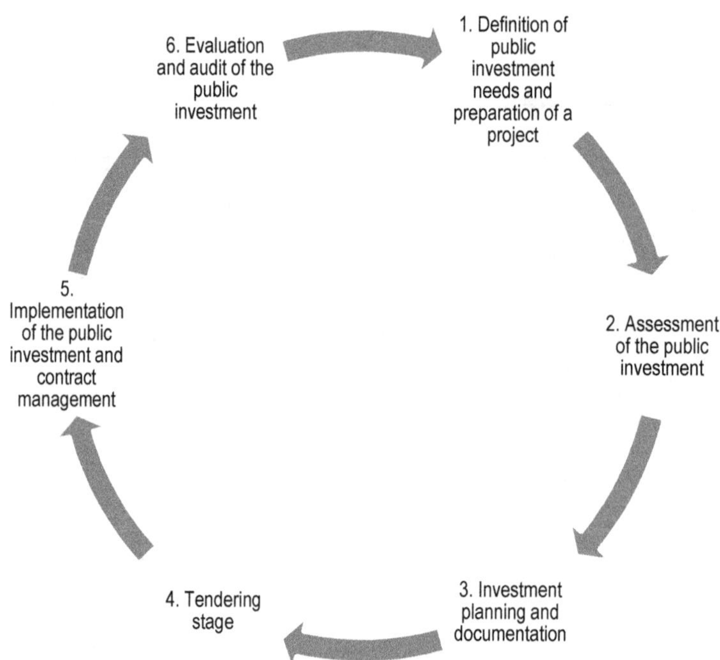

Source: OECD (2016[2]), *Integrity Framework for Public Investment*, OECD Public Governance Reviews, OECD Publishing, Paris, https://doi.org/10.1787/9789264251762-en.

This chapter focuses on the measures in place in Quebec to improve the transparency and accountability of public authorities at the identification of needs and public procurement planning stage. Focusing primarily on infrastructure projects, this chapter also deals more generally with the planning of overall public procurement.

Objective, transparent and politically independent planning of works and infrastructure projects

In response to a recommendation of the Charbonneau Commission, an Independent Expert Committee (IEC) was established by the Ministry of Transportation on 31 March 2016 to provide advice on planning the public procurement for which it is responsible. The IEC's members are three external and independent experts in the fields of engineering, finance and governance.

The objective behind the creation of the IEC is to ensure objectivity in the selection of infrastructure projects and to depoliticise the approval of road conservation and improvement projects at the Ministry of Transportation (CEIC, 2015[3]).

The specific structure of the IEC goes beyond the practices generally put in place in other OECD countries to depoliticise the planning of infrastructure projects, and to our knowledge does not appear to have any equivalent. Best practice in OECD countries to increase government accountability in needs identification and planning of infrastructure projects focuses more on specific projects rather than on processes for overall road infrastructure programming (Box 2.1).

Box 2.1. The Public and Private Infrastructure Investment Management Centre (PIMAC) in Korea

The PIMAC is a think tank that evaluates projects in the context of Preliminary Feasibility Studies (PFS) and conducts feasibility reassessments of public investments as well as profitability tests of PPP projects involving infrastructure investments.

The Guidelines for Preliminary Feasibility Studies provide guidance on how to assess projects and what type of cost-benefit analysis should be included. The aim is to present the results of the technical assessment work logically and clearly, to ensure consistency between the individual Preliminary Feasibility Studies and to improve the reliability and accountability of their results. These are general and standardised principles applicable to each area concerned: roads, railways, airports, ports, culture, tourism, sports and research and development.

These principles give precise indications on economic feasibility, assessment of budgetary feasibility, public policy analysis (e.g. the degree of regional development, promotion of the regional economy, eligibility for budget support, consistency with related programmes, environmental impact assessment, etc.) and the analytical hierarchy process (AHP).

Source: (OECD, 2016[2]).

Since its inception, the IEC has submitted two reports - for the 2017-19 road planning (IEC, 2017[4]) and the 2018-20 road planning respectively (IEC, 2018[5]). An important aspect of the 2018-2020 report is that it documents progress in implementing the recommendations of the 2017-2019 report. Both are available on the Ministry of Transportation's (MTQ) website, which promotes government transparency and accountability regarding the implementation of the IEC's recommendations. The Ministry has produced an action plan to ensure the implementation of the IEC recommendations, and according to the information shared, it is currently being carried out. It noted that the MTQ ensures rigorous internal monitoring of the progress made in implementing the IEC's recommendations and has set reasonable deadlines for all recommendations.

Formalising the existence of the Independent Experts Committee and the process for following up its recommendations in a law or directive

To date, from the perspective of the MTQ and the Public Monitoring Committee on the recommendations of the Charbonneau Commission (Monitoring Committee), the IEC's work has been successful. The government could formalise its operation in a law or directive if it wants to ensure its sustainability.

Formalising the Independent Experts Committee in a law or directive

According to the MTQ and the Monitoring Committee, the IEC makes a significant contribution to increasing transparency in planning public procurement and the work of the Ministry of Transportation. Since the IEC's mandate was originally limited to two years, it was renewed for another two-year period following a process of appointment of new members by the MTQ. Given the positive results of the IEC's work and the MTQ's desire to renew the IEC's mandate on an ongoing basis, the MTQ could consider formalising the IEC's role and mandate, as well as the monitoring process of the IEC's recommendations, within a law or a directive from the Minister of Transportation. Currently, there is no formal legislative authority or policy on the governance of the IEC in order to increase transparency on the implementation of its recommendations.

However, according to some of the stakeholders interviewed, the publication of these reports goes relatively unnoticed. The MTQ may consider other ways to share updates on the implementation of the IEC's recommendations. Some of the report's findings raise issues of public interest, such as the increasing degradation of Quebec's road network despite increased investment in its maintenance. More frequent publication of the Government's planned actions to address the issues identified by the IEC would enhance transparency and accountability and contribute to public confidence in government.

Mitigating the risk of politicisation of all major public infrastructure projects

The IEC's mandate is limited to infrastructure work for which the MTQ is responsible, but other major infrastructure projects are also vulnerable to the risk of politicisation.

Extending the IEC's mandate to all major public infrastructure projects

There is a limited number of public contracts that are prone to being embezzled in order to acquire political capital at the local level, but this risk is not limited to road infrastructure projects for which the MTQ is responsible. According to the information gathered for this report, investment planning, i.e., the Quebec Infrastructure Plan (QIP), is approved by the Council of Ministers, with the prioritisation of major infrastructure projects carried out by each minister concerned (including those of the MTQ). Projects for the construction or improvement of real estate infrastructure of any kind, such as hospitals, educational institutions or regional service centres, are therefore also likely to be instrumentalised for political purposes, or at least have the appearance of being so.

Thus, the conclusions of the Charbonneau Commission that it is preferable to establish a certain distance between elected officials and infrastructure projects are applicable to the planning of major projects of all public bodies.

With this in mind, the Government of Quebec adopted the *Public Infrastructure Act* on 30 October 2013. This Act establishes the governance rules for planning public infrastructure investments and managing public infrastructure, to achieve a long-term vision and ensure their quality and sustainability.

In this regard, the President of the Treasury Board, who is responsible for enforcing the *Public Infrastructure Act*, is supported by his Under-Secretariat for Public Infrastructure in carrying out this function. The latter is responsible:

- for co-ordinating the process of evaluating and monitoring the state of public infrastructure assets and monitoring their evolution
- for collecting and analysing the investment needs of public bodies
- for developing and implementing the 10-year Quebec Infrastructure Plan (QIP)
- for preparing an annual report on monitoring public funding allocated to infrastructure
- for advising the Treasury Board on planning, approving and managing public infrastructure projects
- for developing and ensuring the implementation of the necessary framework to ensure optimal governance of major public infrastructure projects
- for developing policies, strategies and guidelines on these matters.

Thus, in order to have comprehensive and in-depth knowledge of the infrastructure assets under the responsibility of the Government of Quebec, the main public bodies, as designated in section 3 of the *Public Infrastructure Act*, are required to submit an annual public infrastructure investments management plan (PAGI) to the President of the Treasury Board and to monitor the condition and asset maintenance deficit of the infrastructure assets under their responsibility, including the effect of investments made during the year. The information generated by the PAGI provides the Government of Quebec with an overview of the evolution of the condition and asset maintenance deficit of most public infrastructure assets.

Additionally, the Government of Quebec has created guiding principles for its public infrastructure investments, based on objectives that prioritise maintaining the supply of services to the public over improving services (Treasury Board Secretariat, 2018[6]). Thus, the guiding principles and the PAGI are taken into account in the QIP proposed to the government y the Treasury Board.

This QIP is accompanied by a report on the use of the funds allocated to infrastructure during the previous financial year and a forecast of their use for the current financial year. After analysing the QIP proposed by the Treasury Board and making the necessary changes, if any, the government attaches a final version of the QIP and the PAGI to the estimates tabled in the National Assembly so that they can be studied by the competent parliamentary committee within the framework of the budgetary allocations. Infrastructure projects worth more than USD 50 million that are being considered, planned or under construction, are made public by the Public Infrastructure Sub-Secretariat through a scorecard published on the Treasury Board Secretariat's website. This transparency tool can be found at the following URL: https://www.tresor.gouv.qc.ca/infrastructures-publiques/tableau-de-bord/.

In addition, with respect to the planning, approval and management of infrastructure projects, the government has adopted the *Directive on the Management of Major Public Infrastructure Projects* (the Directive), which provides a framework and rigorous management rules to support the decision-making process of the Council of Ministers for studying, planning and implementing major projects by public bodies and the significant changes that could be applied to them. Thus, this directive provides for the preparation of extensive documentation to support the need identification, the choice of the selected option and the implementation of major projects (preliminary project sheet, feasibility study and business case as well as progress and final reports).

Finally, to strengthen the monitoring of public infrastructure project implementation, the TBS has set up an Infrastructure Project Governance Committee, chaired by the Associate Secretary for Public Infrastructure of the TBS and consisting of permanent members of the TBS and SQI, as well as respondents from the ministries concerned.

Taken as a whole, the governance put in place by the TBS, namely the development and approval processes for the QIP and the PAGI, the Directive and the Public Infrastructure Projects Dashboard, are an innovative means of increasing transparency and accountability in the planning and prioritisation of Government of Quebec infrastructure projects. These processes are aligned with best practice within OECD countries, and may even compare favourably with some of them.

As shown in Figure 2.2 below, many OECD countries are developing a short list of infrastructure projects to be implemented in the medium term (e.g. within one electoral cycle).

Figure 2.2. Existence of a short list of all infrastructure projects to be implemented in the medium-term in OECD countries

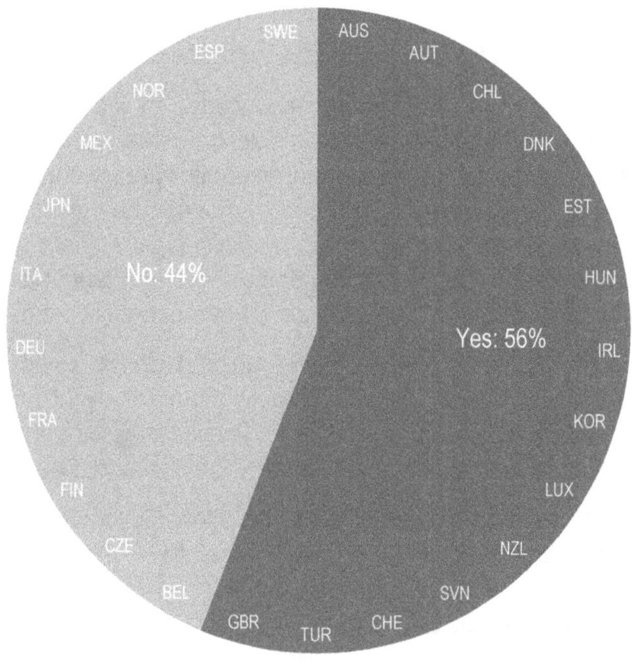

Source: (OECD, 2017[6]).

Comprehensive and transparent planning of infrastructure projects increases the visibility and consistency of project prioritisation, thereby reducing subjective discretionary decisions.

Considering the success achieved by the IEC in support of the MTQ, the fact that the Council of Ministers has the authority to approve and modify the QIP, that the management of the politicisation risk must be updated on a regular basis and that the perspective of external experts could be valuable in this regard, the government could consider how to integrate the IEC's mandate into planning public procurement subject to the *Directive on the Management of Major Public Infrastructure Projects*. The exercise of the IEC's jurisdiction over all major public infrastructure projects could further reduce the appearance of vulnerability to political influences at the expense of governance or technical considerations, and thus increase public confidence in the objectivity of public infrastructure planning.

Strengthening the integrity of public procurement by strengthening and harmonising planning processes

Towards capacity building at the stage of identifying and planning future needs

In the literature, (Schiele, 2007[7]; Barry et al., 1996[8]) the performance of procurement planning has long been recognised as a major component in assessing the strategic maturity of procurement within an organisation. In addition to its impact on the efficiency of public procurement, structured planning minimises the use of non-transparent procedures.

Strengthening the needs planning process to increase transparency and ensure a long-term strategy for the conduct of public procurement

One of the main objectives of the ACPB, as identified in article 2, is to establish “effective and efficient contracting procedures, including careful, thorough evaluation of procurement requirements [...]”. The first step in an in-depth needs assessment is the planning of future needs by procurement officials. In practice, however, this objective is not achieved on a consistent and harmonised basis by all public bodies. Indeed, several stakeholders consulted during the data collection for this report reported a lack of expertise in some public bodies for planning their future needs in a specific and structured way before organising calls for tenders. According to the stakeholders, the lack of expertise in planning for future needs is even more evident in some municipalities, which are governed by the *Cities and Towns Act* and the *Municipal Code*.

The OECD experience shows that certain essential steps must be taken before launching the phase of identifying potential suppliers and analysing their capabilities.[1] First, internal needs must be fully understood to ensure that the market analysis, which will be conducted at a later stage, targets the appropriate products or services.

Procurement planning is not only important for ensuring co-ordinated and efficient operations, but also reducing the unwarranted use of emergency and other exceptions. Nevertheless, this practice is relatively common in public procurement in Quebec, as shown in Figure 2.3.

Figure 2.3. Percentage of procedures used by public bodies above the thresholds for the period 2016-17 and 2015-16

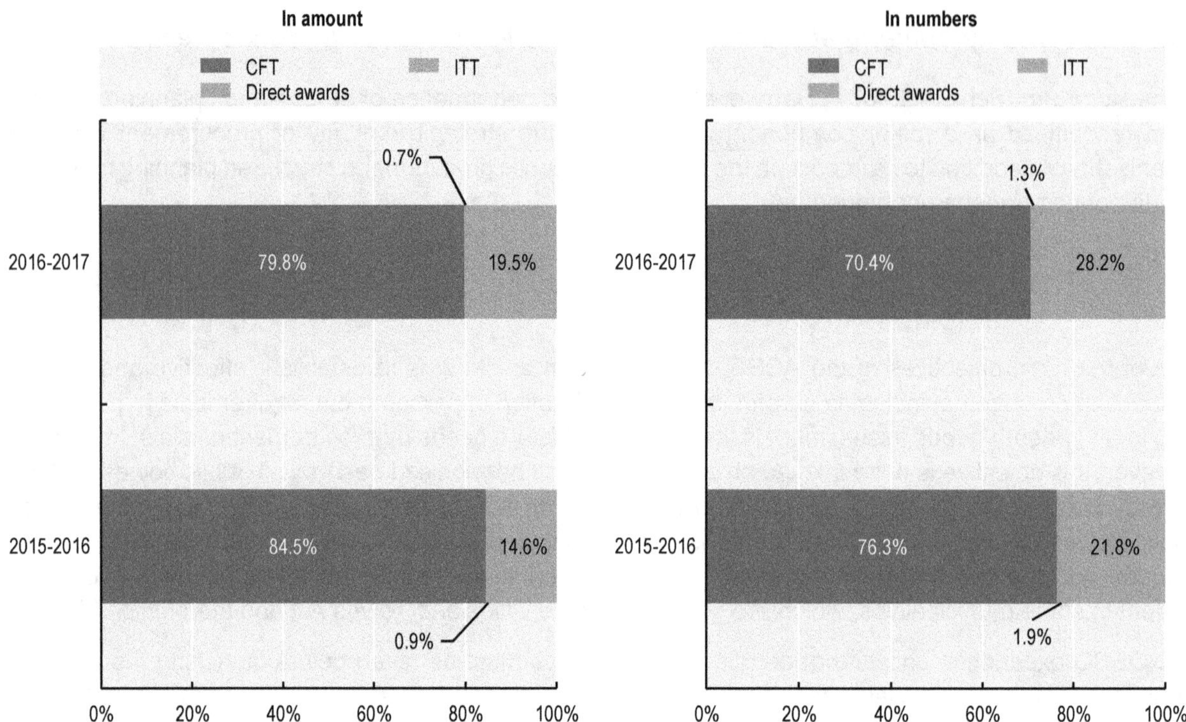

Note: This data does not take account of agreements between public bodies; occupancy agreements entered into with or by the Société québécoise des infrastructures; contracts for the management of the government's real estate holdings; concession contracts for the exercise of a commercial activity on behalf of the government and for which royalties are paid to it; orders for goods resulting from a standing offer agreement, as well as requests for services resulting from an on-call contract.
Source: (Treasury Board Secretariat, 2017[9]).

In addition to reducing the risk of awarding contracts on an exceptional basis thus limiting the transparency of government contracts, procurement planning makes it possible to provide the private sector with an initial list of the needs of public bodies so that they are aware of possible future opportunities. The Government of Quebec has established general guidelines on contract management that include a section on procurement planning. Indeed, the guide *Processus de référence en gestion contractuelle* (Reference procedures for contract management), developed by the CSPQ, provides examples of best practices in order to promote their adoption.

Moreover, as discussed in "Mitigating the risk of politicisation of all major public infrastructure projects" section, the Government of Quebec has implemented a planning and prioritisation process developed for public infrastructure projects. In particular, the Directive requires the production of a feasibility study which must demonstrate the need to enable the Council of Ministers to decide on the relevance of an infrastructure project. The TBS may also require the deputy minister or head of the contracting authority to appoint an individual to co-ordinate the work of a team that provides centralised governance for the management of the public infrastructure project portfolio. As part of its work, the team advises the deputy minister or leader of the public body on the following aspects of public infrastructure projects:

1. identification, selection and prioritisation of projects
2. co-ordination and monitoring of projects
3. any other aspect as determined by the Treasury Board.

The Government of Quebec also organises reverse technology showcases, which require a structured procurement planning process by allowing public bodies to communicate their future information technology needs. These meetings, which are public and open to all businesses, allow them to obtain relevant information and adapt the design of their solutions to the needs of future government projects.

In a similar vein, procurement planning practices are implemented in a structured and permanent way in many OECD countries, as demonstrated in Chapter 4, and also serve to increase levels of competition in public procurement, thus indirectly limiting their exposure to corruption risks. However, the nature of the information published must be carefully assessed to ensure that increased transparency on the future needs of the public sector does not give rise to another type of corruption risk: collusion (OECD, 2012[10]).

Beyond the development of guidelines, the Government of Quebec is aware of the difficulties faced by public servants in establishing and following rigorous processes for the identification of needs prior to the development and submission phase of calls for tenders, and is therefore developing two centres of expertise. One of these centres will focus on public markets in the construction sector and will be led by the Société québécoise des infrastructures (SQI). The other centre will focus on purchasing information technology and will be led by the Centre de services partagés du Québec (CSPQ). Considering that these centres of expertise are expected to cover the entire contract management cycle, the SQI and the CSPQ could pay particular attention to the supervision of public bodies at the identification of needs stage.

A third centre of expertise dealing with contract management at municipal level has also been created. It was developed by the Ministry of Municipal Affairs and Housing (MAMH) in collaboration with the Fédération québécoise des municipalités (FQM) and the Union des municipalités du Québec (UMQ). It includes three working groups that share five priorities, namely: 1) identification of needs; 2) method of award; 3) call for tenders; 4) contract award; and 5) contract monitoring. According to the MAMH, the identification of needs was recognised as a priority, given that lack of knowledge sometimes makes it difficult to identify the optimal project, even though this step is essential to developing tender documents. In addition, too little attention is paid to the identification of needs, which results in a proliferation of addenda and changes in the guidelines, and can seriously undermine the credibility of a project. A lack of knowledge and interest in a rigorous definition process can also make a project more vulnerable to undue influence from third parties.

Although the Government of Quebec has implemented concrete measures to strengthen the needs planning process, their application is limited to certain types of public procurement, such as those in the infrastructure and information technology sector. Thus, the government could consider further strengthening its guidance at the stage of identifying and defining the needs of public bodies. For example, to complement the guidelines on procurement planning, the TBS could provide technical resources to support all public bodies in the application of best practices and requirements applicable to specific contexts. The benefits associated with consolidating technical expertise are also discussed in the "Providing support to municipalities and municipal officials in matters of integrity and public procurement" section in chapter 1.

More institutionalised planning would enhance the accountability of public procurement decisions and facilitate audits

In addition, the Government of Quebec could establish specific standards for documentation of the decision making process with respect to the identification of needs by public and municipal bodies. For its part, the MAMH supports the municipal community by helping it to establish its own standards. Although requirements exist for documentation to support Council of Ministers decisions in the infrastructure sector (see "Objective, transparent and politically independent planning of works and infrastructure projects" section), they do not consistently apply to all procurement by public and municipal bodies. Indeed, according to discussions with stakeholders for this report, audit results from the Quebec Auditor General revealed that some of the planning processes for public procurement in sectors other than infrastructure were poorly or not at all documented, particularly in relation to the cost estimates for public procurement. The examples of New Zealand and Croatia below help us to understand some of the benefits of formally publishing procurement plans, particularly with regard to audits (Box 2.2).

Box 2.2. Publication of procurement plans

New Zealand

In New Zealand, the Annual Procurement Plans of government agencies are made public. They contain an indicative list of contracts envisaged over the next twelve months and should be sent to the Ministry of Business, Innovation and Employment (MBIE). The Ministry then publishes the procurement plans as a consolidated list on its website. In addition to an annual plan, government organisations must also submit an Extended Procurement Forecast (EPF) and a Significant Procurement Plan (SPP) to the Ministry for the following contracts:

- Contracts with an estimated total value of more than NZD 5 million over the life of the contract.
- Contracts that, due to their nature or complexity, could expose the government to significant risks if they are not performed according to original specifications, within budget and on time.
- Contracts that potentially involve inter-governmental collaboration or resource sharing.

The EPF is a list of the contracts planned for the next 4 years, while the SPP gives more details on the contracts the agency intends to enter into, how it wishes to carry out the process, the method used for awarding the contract and the evaluation of bids. The SSP must be reviewed by the MBIE, which in turn provides the public body with comments and advice on the content of the plan, its consistency with public procurement rules, the appropriate assessment of costs and risks, the types of contracts envisaged, and the areas in which the development of supply capacity should be concentrated. This assessment enables bodies to improve procurement planning, better optimise resources over the life of the contracts and identify opportunities for collaboration with other bodies. It must inevitably be taken into account by the public body.

Croatia

In Croatia, the publication of annual procurement plans started with the implementation of the European Structural and Investment Funds. Specifically, contracting authorities are required to publish their annual procurement plans online within 60 days of the approval of their budgets. This obligation exists for all contracts worth EUR 2 600 or more. Procurement plans are updated every six months.

After an attempt to eliminate procurement planning, this obligation was reintroduced in 2008 as it plays an important role in transparency and auditing purposes. The State Auditor verifies the procurement plan against actual procurement expenditures based on data from the contract registry. If differences arise, the audit authorities request justification. There are no formal sanctions for contracting authorities that go beyond the planned expenditure, but the audit authorities may carry out further investigations if the divergences from the original plan have not been sufficiently justified.

Procurement plans also allow audit authorities to verify whether the value of the procurement contracts has been split. As a result, contracting authorities are more accountable for their actions.

Procurement planning also has a professionalising effect on contracting authorities, since they are asked to forecast their needs and align the expenditure allocated to them with their policy objectives. For example, a procurement plan helps to demonstrate how policy objectives are linked to operational actions, i.e. projects implemented through public procurement.

Source: Adapted from (European Commission, n.d.[11]; Government of New Zealand, 2015[12]).

In view of the shortcomings identified at this stage of public procurement, the government could encourage internal and external audit bodies, all while respecting their autonomy, to include the process of identification of needs and procurement planning in their audits on a regular basis. An increased role for auditors in this phase would allow the implementation of a monitoring mechanism to ensure that projects are actually implemented in accordance with the plans of public bodies. This could strengthen the integrity of the planning process by enhancing accountability.

Finally, Quebec could draw on the experiences of many OECD countries where there is co-ordination of projects at both national and regional levels (Australia, Korea, Italy, Japan, New Zealand, United Kingdom, Sweden, and Turkey) to better co-ordinate the conduct of public procurement by the various levels of government. (Box 2.3).

Box 2.3. Infrastructure Australia and the Platform for Dialogue between National and Sub-national Government Levels

Infrastructure Australia

In 2008, the central government established the advisory body Infrastructure Australia (IA) to co-ordinate with the states on investments of national importance. This body advises the central government on investment priorities in the transport, communications, water and energy sectors and assists the states in identifying national infrastructure priorities. IA adjudicates state applications for funding under the Building Australia Fund (BAF), the main national funding mechanism for major infrastructure projects.

Platform for dialogue between the national and sub-national public levels

The Council of Australian Governments (COAG) is the main body responsible for defining and implementing inter-institutional co-operation policy. The members of the COAG are the Prime Minister, state and territory Premiers, and the President of the Australian Local Government Association. Within the COAG, federal and sub-national governments have endorsed national guidelines on public-private partnerships, agreed on a national ports strategy and entered into inter-agency agreements on heavy vehicles, railways and marine safety. The COAG also receives regular reports from Infrastructure Australia.

Source: (OECD, 2016[2]).

Harmonising processes to increase the integration and visibility of future public procurement

Procurement planning processes are generally not harmonised or co-ordinated across public bodies. This can have a negative impact on accountability and the costs entailed by public procurement.

Harmonising planning processes across public bodies to increase the integration and visibility of future public procurement processes

Within all contracting authorities (CA) surveyed, public procurement planning is generally conducted in a decentralised manner by the operational units or by the territorial directorates-general. However, there are some variations from one organisation to another. For example, the main organiser of public procurement at the RAMQ, the information technology directorate, submits an annual plan to the public contracts management body. But for the other directorates, intentions to organise public procurement processes are channelled in an *ad hoc* manner. There is also no co-ordination between public and municipal agencies wishing to tender simultaneously for a given contract.

Firstly, a lack of central planning co-ordination can affect transparency and accountability in an organisation's procurement process. For example, the Territorial Directorates General (TDG) prepare their proposed planning on the basis of intervention strategies and guidelines for the choice of projects to be prioritised, as established by central government. In the interests of efficiency and transparency, the IEC recently recommended that the MTQ examine the possibility of preparing a "suggested" plan for the entire province at central level, which could then be sent to the TDGs for validation (IEC, 2017[4]). The TDGs could then make changes to the plan based on the characteristics of their region. The objective behind this recommendation is to "facilitate the transparency and documentation of changes, deletions, amendments or additions introduced to meet regional particularities" (IEC, 2017[4]). In its 2018 report, the IEC also proposes that the MTQ's central organisation follow up with the TDGs on the preparation of projects before the planning, which could be used to identify any observable discrepancies between projects under development and departmental priorities earlier, and thus make corrections more quickly. Article 17 of the *Public Infrastructure Act* allows the TBS to require the deputy minister or head of the contracting authority to designate a team responsible for co-ordinating the centralised management of public infrastructure projects, including: 1) the identification, selection and prioritisation of projects; 2) the co-ordination and monitoring of projects; and 3) any other aspect determined by the TBS.

As mentioned earlier, a lack of co-ordination and planning of the various public procurement processes may require undue use of exceptions to the tendering process, which may increase costs and conceal any wrongdoings. Firms that regularly participate in calls for tenders report that there is no analysis at the government or municipal level of the ability of individual markets to meet the demand from one or more simultaneous calls for tenders in a given region (see also the discussion on market analysis in Chapter 3). Excessive demand in relation to the market's ability to meet it can lead to significant price increases and the need to resort to lower quality proposals. More integrated planning of the needs of public bodies would result in fewer calls for tenders being issued within the same market for a given period, which could have a positive impact on price and quality.

The Government of Quebec could therefore consider harmonising procurement planning processes so that they are consistent between various public bodies. The MAMH may consider doing the same for municipal agencies. These harmonised processes require better planning of decentralised units within each public agency, to have more integrated central planning at the level of public bodies. The Government of Quebec could be inspired by best practices implemented by some OECD countries, such as New Zealand and Italy (Box 2.4). Indeed, after several cases of public procurement wrongdoings exposed in the media, Italy has merged its public procurement authority into its anti-corruption agency (ANAC) and has extended the applicable powers of monitoring and intervention. As a result, Consip currently has robust and detailed procedures for procurement planning and market analysis.

Unplanned public procurement processes could remain possible in Quebec with sufficient justification, so that these procedures become the exception rather than the rule in all public bodies. With consolidated information on the future needs of the public sector, the Government of Québec could also put in place a strategic approach and a process to co-ordinate the carrying out of public procurement by various public and municipal bodies, so that it can assess the capacity of markets to meet demand.

Box 2.4. Centralisation and harmonisation of planning processes

New Zealand

In New Zealand, the publication by government agencies of two additional procurement plans, alongside annual procurement plans, is intended to enable the government to facilitate cross-government planning. The first 4-year plan (Extended Procurement Forecast, EPF) provides a long-term vision of the procurement envisaged by government agencies, while the second plan (Significant Procurement Plan, SPP) allows central government to identify synergies and opportunities for collaboration.

The latter objective is part of a reform of the government's public procurement policy implemented in 2012 (Procurement Functional Leadership, PFL), which has led to savings and efficiency gains through the establishment of various collaborative contracts under the management of the Minister of Business, Innovation and Employment (MBIE). Collaborative contracts allow government bodies to achieve cost savings through economies of scale, alignment of business needs, savings on transaction costs and establishment of common contract and governance frameworks.

Recognising the potential benefits of this approach, a growing number of government bodies are taking part in these contracts. According to the 2014 Activity Report of the PFL, more than 720 agencies participate in "All-of-Government Contracts" (AoGs), a type of collaborative contract that establishes procurement agreements with approved suppliers for certain common goods or services purchased across government. Total expected savings over the life of all AoG contracts also increased from USD 348 million to USD 415.1 million. This centralised process has enabled the Government to influence strategic procurement and strengthen leadership at the central level, in addition to achieving cost savings through the consolidation of spending.

Italy

The Sourcing Activities Plan (SAP) is a general plan that the Purchasing Department of Consip, the Italian national agency in charge of public procurement, uses to plan and supervise its annual activity. It allows for a better matching of procurement phases to resources and procurement lead times. It indicates the complexity of the planned contract, the category manager responsible for it, the start and end month of each major phase, and the expected availability date of the contract.

Depending on the complexity of the contract concerned (low, medium or high), different implementation times are estimated, ranging from two to three months for the market analysis and feasibility study, and from six to nine months for the tendering strategy and the drafting of all documents.

The SAP is intended for internal use, but the estimated date of contract availability is published on the national electronic procurement portal to help buyers and suppliers prepare for contracting.

Source: Consip SpA.

Action plan

Transparent planning that is independent of political considerations

- Formalising the Independent Experts Committee in a law or directive
- Extending the IEC's mandate to all major public infrastructure projects

Strengthening and harmonising planning processes in public bodies

- Strengthening the needs planning process to increase transparency and ensure a long-term strategy for the conduct of public procurement
- Institutionalising planning processes to strengthen the accountability of public procurement decisions and facilitate audits
- Harmonising planning processes across public bodies to increase the integration and visibility of future public procurement processes

References

Barry, J. et al. (1996), "A Development Model for Effective MRO Procurement", *International Journal of Purchasing and Materials Management*, Vol. 32/2, pp. 35-44, http://dx.doi.org/10.1111/j.1745-493X.1996.tb00284.x. [8]

CEIC (2015), *Rapport final de la Commission d'enquête sur l'octroi et la gestion des contrats publics dans l'industrie de la construction*, https://www.ceic.gouv.qc.ca/fileadmin/Fichiers_client/fichiers/Rapport_final/Rapport_final_CEIC_Integral_c.pdf. [3]

European Commission (n.d.), *Increasing the quality of public procurement: Publish annual procurement plans*, http://ec.europa.eu/regional_policy/sources/good_practices/GP_fiche_12.pdf (accessed on 13 May 2020). [11]

Government of New Zealand (2015), *Government Rules of Sourcing: Rules for planning your procurement, approaching the market and contracting*, Government of New Zealand, Public procurement, https://www.procurement.govt.nz/assets/procurement-property/documents/government-rules-of-sourcing-procurement.pdf. [12]

IEC (2018), *Avis du Comité d'experts indépendants*, Independent Experts Committee, https://www.transports.gouv.qc.ca/fr/projets-infrastructures/investissements/investissements-routiers/investissements-routiers-2018-2020/Documents/avis-programmation.pdf. [5]

IEC (2017), *Avis du Comité d'experts indépendants*, Independent Experts Committee, https://www.transports.gouv.qc.ca/fr/projets-infrastructures/investissements/investissements-routiers/investissements-routiers-2017-2019/Documents/comite_experts_final.pdf. [4]

OECD (2017), *Getting Infrastructure Right: A framework for better governance*, OECD Publishing, Paris, https://dx.doi.org/10.1787/9789264272453-en. [6]

OECD (2016), *Integrity Framework for Public Investment*, OECD Public Governance Reviews, OECD Publishing, Paris, https://dx.doi.org/10.1787/9789264251762-en. [2]

OECD (2014), *OECD Foreign Bribery Report: An Analysis of the Crime of Bribery of Foreign Public Officials*, OECD Publishing, Paris, https://dx.doi.org/10.1787/9789264226616-en. [1]

OECD (2012), *OECD Recommendation of the Council on Fighting Bid Rigging in Public Procurement*, OECD, Paris, https://www.oecd.org/daf/competition/RecommendationOnFightingBidRigging2012.pdf. [10]

Schiele, H. (2007), "Supply-management maturity, cost savings and purchasing absorptive capacity: Testing the procurement-performance link", *Journal of Purchasing & Supply Management*, Vol. 13, pp. 274-293, http://dx.doi.org/10.1016/j.pursup.2007.10.002. [7]

Treasury Board Secretariat (2018), *Balises à l'égard des exigences et des critères contractuels en services profesionnels liés à la construction*, https://www.tresor.gouv.qc.ca/fileadmin/PDF/faire_affaire_avec_etat/Balise_construction_services_professionnels.pdf (accessed on 24 July 2018). [14]

Treasury Board Secretariat (2018), *Entreprises inscrites au RENA*, https://rena.tresor.gouv.qc.ca/rena/rechercher.aspx?type=lettre&lettre=a-z (accessed on 27 July 2018). [13]

Treasury Board Secretariat (2017), "Statistiques sur les contrats des organismes publics 2016-2017", https://www.tresor.gouv.qc.ca/fileadmin/PDF/faire_affaire_avec_etat/statistiques/1617.pdf (accessed on 18 July 2018). [9]

Note

[1] Presentations made during an OECD workshop on improving public procurement practices at the Institute for Social Security and State Workers' Services (ISSSTE), 2-4 September 2014, Mexico City, by experts from Chile, Denmark, Portugal and the United Kingdom.

3 The use of competitive public procurement in Quebec

The integrity of the contract management system is directly related to the modes of procurement used by public and municipal bodies that require different degrees of competition, but also to the selection and award criteria chosen, which may be restrictive or manipulated in order to award a public contract to a given supplier. Moreover, integrity cannot be assessed without analysing the level of transparency of the system and its digitisation in terms of procedures and access to information and various documents throughout the contract management cycle. The purpose of this chapter is therefore to analyse the system in place in Quebec in terms of procurement methods, selection and award criteria and transparency, and to provide recommendations on measures to strengthen the integrity of the contract management system.

Ensuring an honest, effective and efficient contract management system is based on fair access to public procurement opportunities for potential competitors of all sizes but also on an adequate degree of transparency. The OECD Recommendation on Public Procurement stresses the importance of competition and of limiting the use of exceptions and single-source procurement, as well as the importance of defining relevant criteria for the award of contracts (selection and award process). Indeed, the risks of integrity violations are also linked to public procurement methods and to the award criteria used by public authorities (OECD, 2015[1]). An adequate degree of transparency in contract management not only promotes accountability and ensures access to information, but also plays an important role in levelling the playing field for businesses, thereby limiting the risk of integrity violations (OECD, 2016[2]).

Towards the use of appropriate contract management procedures

As in the contract management systems of OECD countries and elsewhere, there are three types of procedures in Quebec: "the call for tenders (CFT)", which is the general procedure used, "the invitation to tender", ITT and direct award contracts (DCA). Given the impact of each of these procedures on the integrity of the system and on competition in a given market, each method used needs to be justified in specific cases (OECD, 2019[3]). Indeed, less competitive procedures present a greater risk of integrity violations if they are not properly used and controlled.

Towards more competitive procurement procedures below the calls for tenders thresholds

In Quebec, different CFT thresholds can be applied because public and municipal bodies are subject to different procurement liberalisation agreements. The thresholds therefore vary according to the status of the different bodies and whether or not the contracts are for supplies, services, information technology, or construction work. A significant portion of the purchases undertaken by public and municipal bodies are below the CFT threshold, so it is important to ensure that a competitive environment is created below the thresholds to limit the risk of integrity violations.

Promoting competitive procedures below the thresholds by introducing an intermediate threshold above which entities must use the ITT

Below the CFT thresholds, Quebec's regulatory framework ensures sound contract management by imposing a number of mechanisms on public bodies, including the possibility of:

- proceeding by CFT or ITT
- competitor rotation
- putting in place control provisions related to the total value of the contract and any additional expenditure
- establishing a monitoring mechanism to ensure the effectiveness and efficiency of the procedures used
- introducing, subject to any applicable cross-governmental agreement, measures promoting the procurement of goods, services, or construction works from competitors or contractors in the region concerned.

This last point reflects a major issue in Quebec that is common to several OECD countries: the economic development of small and medium-sized enterprises - local SMEs, and SMEs in remote regions.

Accordingly, each public entity has internal regulations indicating the procedures to be followed in accordance with its principles. Prior to 1st January 2018, municipal agencies were able to award contracts directly if the amount was less than USD 25 000; and by invitation to at least two suppliers if the amount was between USD 25 000 and USD 100 000. Since then, municipal bodies are able to put in place any rules they wish for the award of contracts involving expenditure of less than USD 100 000 as long as they adopt regulations on contract management specifying the circumstances in which these different modes will apply. Given that each entity defines the procedures to be followed in its rules of procedure, the rules may differ from one entity to another, which impacts the clarity of the regulatory framework for suppliers and increases the risk of integrity violations. For example, for a professional services contract, the TBS may use direct award contracts when the estimated amount is less than USD 50 000, whereas the Ministry of Transportation, Sustainable Mobility and Transport Electrification must prioritise the ITT up to USD 89 999. According to data for public bodies, for procedures below the thresholds and above USD 25 000, although the different regulatory frameworks require bodies to assess the possibility of proceeding by CFT or ITT, the use of direct awards is much more widespread. Indeed, below the thresholds for the period 2016-17, CFTs represent only 18% of the amount of the procedures, ITT 22.5% while DCAs represent more than 59.6% of these procedures (Figure 3.1).

Figure 3.1. Percentage of procedures used by public bodies below the thresholds for the period 2016-17 and 2015-16

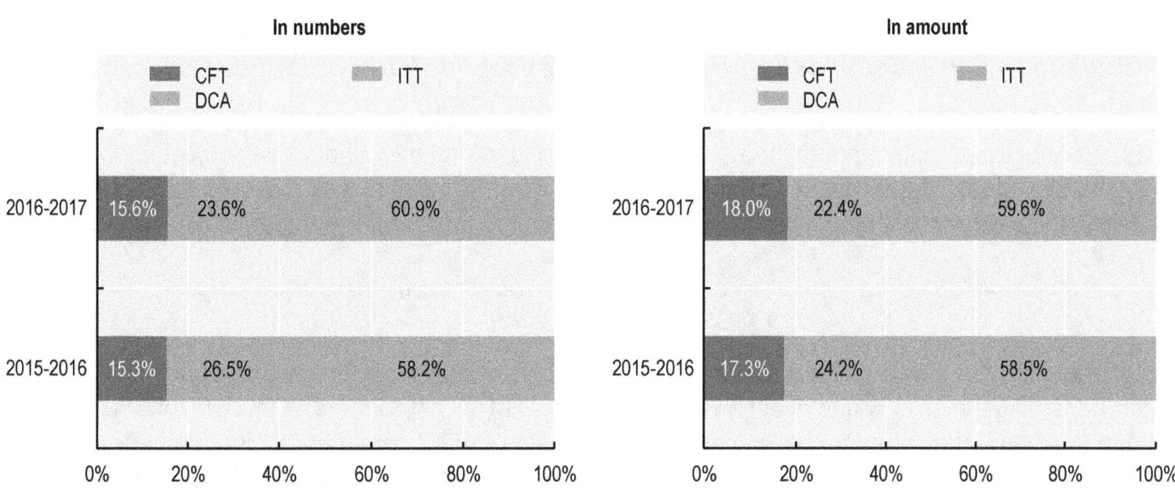

Note: This data does not take account of agreements between public bodies; occupancy agreements entered into with or by the Société québécoise des infrastructures; contracts for the management of the government's real estate holdings; concession contracts for the exercise of a commercial activity on behalf of the government and for which royalties are paid to it; orders for goods resulting from a standing offer agreement, as well as requests for services resulting from an on-call contract.
Source: (Treasury Board Secretariat, 2017[4]).

To promote more competitive procedures below the thresholds but also to promote the integrity of the system, some OECD countries have introduced two thresholds, one above which the public entity must use the CFT, and one above which it must use a competitive and simplified procedure such as the ITT. Beyond the regulatory framework, it is necessary to support contracting authorities by providing them with clear guides or guidelines on the choice of procedure and the steps to be followed. Box 3.1 describes the system in place in Ireland, which has established guidelines applicable to all public bodies in order to inform them about which procedure should be followed according to each value. The Government of Quebec could therefore consider standardising the rules on the method of awarding contracts below the thresholds by developing guidelines to promote competitive procedures and by encouraging public and municipal bodies to introduce a harmonised intermediate threshold above which entities should be able to use the ITT.

Box 3.1. Below-threshold procedures in Ireland

In Ireland, the Office of Public Procurement (OPP) has developed guidelines to promote best practices and consistent enforcement of the rules for the procurement of goods and services. One of the issues covered by these guidelines is procedures below the thresholds where different procedures are prescribed according to the following estimated amounts:

- less than EUR 5 000 excluding VAT: contracts may be awarded following verbal quotes from one or more potential suppliers
- between EUR 5 000 and EUR 25 000 excluding VAT: contracts may be awarded following written tenders submitted by at least three potential suppliers
- between EUR 25 000 excluding VAT and the European CFT threshold: contracts must be published as a formal procedure.

Source: (Office of Government Procurement, 2017[5]).

Harmonisation and rationalisation of the use of exceptions to competitive procedures

In order to limit the use of exceptions to the CFT, international best practice emphasises that such exceptions should be limited, predefined and duly justified, and that they should be subject to appropriate control that would take into account the increased risk of integrity violations. A clear regulatory framework concerning the use of these exceptions is therefore important for both public entities and the private sector.

Providing clear rules and guidelines for the use of all exceptions, particularly for the concepts of "confidentiality and protected information"

As in all regulatory frameworks for public procurement, Quebec has provided for exceptions to the CFT in specific cases. Agencies may use direct award contracts or ITT as appropriate. Although certain cases are common to several regulatory frameworks in OECD and non-OECD countries, they nevertheless require clear rules or guidelines to limit abuse of these exceptions. For example, in Quebec there is no regulatory framework defining the concepts of "confidentiality" or "protected information" in the context of public procurement. The OECD experience in several countries, including countries of the European Union and Norway, has shown that one of the main problems encountered by public officials relates to the definition of the term "confidential". Characterising a procedure as confidential in order to award a contract to a specific supplier has a negative impact on the perception of public procurement as an open and fair process (OECD, 2019[3]). Therefore, to ensure the effectiveness and integrity of the system, the use of this exception requires clear rules and definitions. The Government of Quebec could provide a clear definition and guidelines for the concepts of "confidentiality" and "protected information" to limit the abuse of these exceptions. Box 3.2 describes international best practices for procedures that have confidential aspects.

Box 3.2. Public procurement process and confidentiality

In many countries, legislation provides for different levels of classification of confidential information. Depending on the classification of the documents concerned and the need to make certain information public before tenders are submitted, public bodies may:

- award the contract directly through a direct contract (where the information is highly confidential)
- use a restricted CFT process, during which participating suppliers must sign a Confidentiality and Non-Disclosure Agreement to protect confidential information; or
- use an open tendering process but disclose confidential information only to the successful bidder.

Source: (OECD, 2019[3]).

Promoting more competition for CFT exceptions

A provision was introduced in the ACPB in 2017 for some specific exceptions, stating that a public body may award the contract following an invitation to tender when more than one contractor is available. More than ten cases are provided for in government regulations. This provision will therefore have a positive effect on competition and the integrity of the system. Indeed, as shown in the figure below, for the period 2016-17 (before the entry into force of this new provision), contracts awarded directly and by ITT represented, respectively, 19.5% and 0.7% of the total number of processes above the thresholds (which are therefore exceptions). This shows that ITT was not the preferred award method. For the period 2017-18, the number of ITT procedures increased to 4.4%, while direct awards decreased to 16.9%. These figures only partially reflect the benefits of the new provision, as it was not actually implemented until February 2018. The Government of Quebec should therefore continue its efforts to improve competition in awarding public contracts and to implement actions, such as further promoting ITTs, which is a more competitive procedure than direct awards.

Figure 3.2. Percentage of procedures used by public bodies above the thresholds for the period 2016-17 and 2015-16

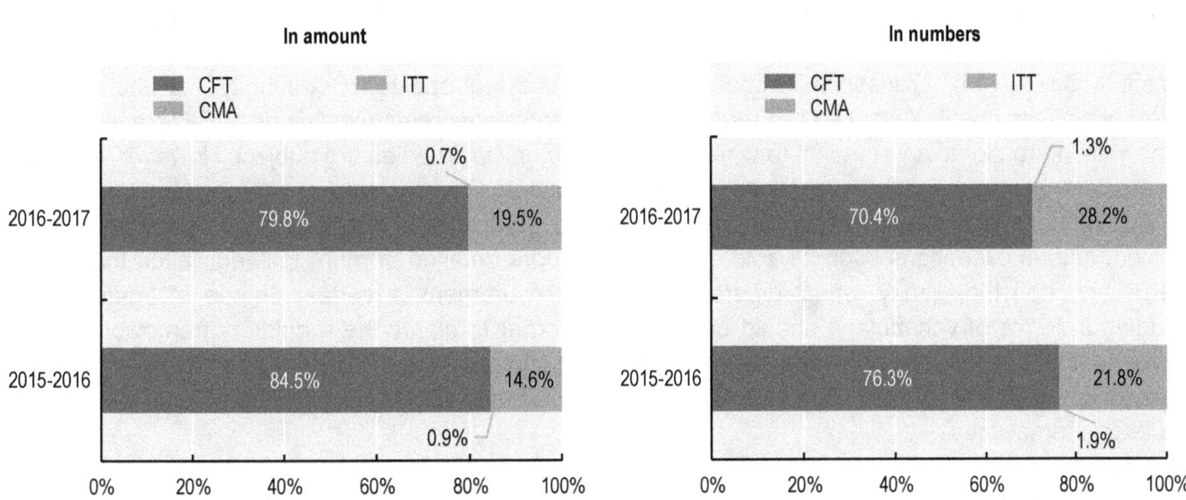

Note: This data does not take account of agreements between public bodies; occupancy agreements entered into with or by the Société québécoise des infrastructures; contracts for the management of the government's real estate holdings; concession contracts for the exercise of a commercial activity on behalf of the government and for which royalties are paid to it; orders for goods resulting from a standing offer agreement, as well as requests for services resulting from an on-call contract.
Source: (Treasury Board Secretariat, 2017[4]).

In addition, with respect to the exceptional cases provided for in the regulatory framework, the Government of Quebec could the following ones by way of a CFT or ITT:

- contracts for legal services - ACPB and its regulations
- financial or banking services contracts - ACPB and its regulations.

Indeed, although the regulatory framework allows a public body to enter into direct award contracts, this does not prevent it from using a more competitive procedure such as the ITT or the CFT. However, these sectors are sufficiently competitive for these procedures to be conducted by CFTs. For example, in the Quebec business register, more than 500 businesses engage in activities related to legal services. In addition, in very specific and justified cases, such as contracts requiring a high degree of confidentiality or very specialised legal or banking services, a public body could even use the "confidentiality" or "sole sourcing" exception. Countries such as the United Kingdom have put in place multi-attribute framework agreements to meet this type of need in order to promote competition and limit the risk of integrity violations (Box 3.3).

Box 3.3. Advantages of the framework agreement on legal services in the United Kingdom

A framework agreement has been put in place by the Crown Commercial Service, the United Kingdom's central purchasing agency, for the provision of legal advisory services for central government public entities. There is no minimum or maximum value limit for the use of the framework agreement; however, contracts with a value of less than GBP 20 000 may be exempted. The suppliers of the framework agreement are divided into two categories according to their size and degree of expertise.

The use of this framework agreement has provided public bodies with several advantages and benefits: competitive rates, ease of use, supplier relationship management, and extended scope.

Source: adapted from (Crown Commercial Service, 2017[6]).

Harmonising exceptions to CFTs between the regulatory frameworks for public and municipal bodies

For public bodies in Quebec, exceptions are provided for in the ACPB but also in its regulations. For municipal bodies, all exceptions are provided for in the relevant legislation (Cities and Towns Act (CTA), Municipal Code (CM), Transport Companies Act, Quebec Metropolitan Community Act and Montreal Metropolitan Community Act). The two regulatory frameworks governing exceptions to CFTs appear to be in line with international agreements to which public and municipal bodies are subject. However, there are some differences between the exceptions in the two regulatory frameworks. For example, the CTA, unlike the ACPB, does not provide exceptions for emergency situations or for reasons of confidentiality. In addition, certain exceptions such as sole sourcing are more detailed in municipal legislation than in the ACPB. Although these may reflect different types of procurement, a certain degree of homogeneity, including in terms of vocabulary, should be ensured in order to clarify the regulatory framework for the private sector, thus fostering the competitive environment and reducing the risks of integrity violations. The Government of Quebec should conduct a study to harmonise the exceptions to CFTs between the different regulatory frameworks.

Making a clear distinction between exceptions to CFTs and those falling under debarments and exemptions from the regulatory framework for public procurement

In addition to exceptions to CFT procedures, several regulatory frameworks in OECD countries also provide for debarments and exemptions from the public procurement framework. The exclusions generally relate to certain categories of purchases or expenditures that cannot fall under the scope of the public procurement legal framework because of transactions that do not correspond to a typical public procurement process. However, these exclusions still need to follow the principles of the regulatory framework. The exemptions relate to how the law applies to public and municipal bodies, including those that are not required to strictly follow the regulatory framework (OECD, 2019[3]). Quebec's regulatory framework provides only for exceptions to the CFT procedures and does not clearly distinguish between cases of exclusions or exemptions as in many regulations governing public contracts. For example, supply, service, construction or information technology contracts for the activities on foreign soil of a delegation general, a delegation or another form of representation of Quebec abroad are considered exclusions in many OECD regulations. The Government of Quebec would benefit from a clear distinction between procedures falling under exceptions to CFTs and those falling under exclusions and exemptions to the regulatory framework for public procurement. Box 3.4 provides an example of procedures excluded from the regulatory framework for public procurement in France.

Box 3.4. The exclusions of the French Public Procurement Code

Part V of the French Public Procurement Code which entered into force on 1 April 2019 contains a list of exclusions applicable to public contracts (Part V, title I, chapter II). Some contracts are not subject to the provisions of the Code, notably:

- **For reasons relating to the status of the contractor**: in the context of a public service contract, when a contractor enjoys an exclusive right, i.e. when it is entrusted by a legislative or regulatory act with a mandate of general interest (Article L2512-4).
- **For reasons relating to the scope of the contract**: public procurement contracts for services regarding the acquisition or rental of real estate, research and development, arbitration and conciliation, services relating to passenger transport by rail or metro, certain financial services and services which are loan contracts, certain legal services, public contracts requiring secrecy or special security measures, and contracts relating to electronic communications, are not subject to the provisions of the Code (Articles L2512-3, L2512-5 et L2513-2).
- **For reasons relating to the scope of the contract and the status of the co-contractor**: certain emergency services awarded to a non-profit organisation or association as well as public procurement contracts awarded to radio or audiovisual service providers are excluded from the scope of application of the Code (Articles L2512-5 ; L2513-1).
- **For reasons relating to the scope of the contract and activity of the contracting authority:** public service contracts awarded by a contracting authority providing postal services, radio or audiovisual communication services, carrying out exploration activities in a geographical area for the purpose of oil and gas prospecting and exploration, or network operators are excluded from the scope of application of the Code (L2513-1, L2513-3, L2513-4, L2513-5).
- **For reasons relating to the enforcement of a procedure provided for in an international agreement or specific to an international organisation** (Articles L2512- 1 et L2512-2).

Source: adapted from (Government of France, 2019[7]).

Continuing efforts to enhance controls over the use of exceptions to competitive procedures

According to the regulatory framework, most exceptions to competitive procedures (sole sourcing, confidentiality, public interest), must be justified and authorised by the head of the public/municipal body. These bodies must put in place control provisions relating to the value of contracts and any related additional expenditure, particularly in the case of procurement through a direct award contract. There is no independent body to review and authorise the use of these exceptions at the level of individual agencies. The TBS exercises its monitoring authority over the SEAO to randomly verify compliance with the rules governing the contracting process, particularly in cases of exceptions to the CFT. Major efforts have been made by Quebec to limit the abuse of exceptions. Thus for 2016-17, 96% of the direct award contracts entered into by the public bodies analysed were justified by the correct legal or regulatory provision. However, the data vary by sector; for example, the figure is 92% for organisations in the health and social services network, which calls for the strengthening of internal controls over the use of exceptions to competitive procedures in order to get closer to attaining 100%.

Using selection and award criteria that prevent bribery and bid-rigging agreements

The choice of selection and award criteria and their respective weightings have a direct impact on competition and also represent an area of high risk in terms of integrity. Indeed, these criteria can be manipulated to award a contract to a particular supplier. Having predictable tender files, in particular the technical specifications and selection and award criteria, also entails a risk of bid-rigging. For this reason, the OECD Council Recommendation on Fighting Bid-Rigging in Public Procurement calls for the adoption of selection criteria designed to enhance the intensity and effectiveness of competition in the award process (OECD, 2012[8]).

Centralising information on supplier performance

Initiatives put in place by different organisations to improve supplier selection can yield more benefits if information is centralised.

Centralised publication of information on supplier performance

In order to obtain a public contract in Quebec, certain eligibility conditions are stipulated in the various laws and regulations depending on the purpose of the contract and its scope. These include holding the necessary qualifications, authorisations, permits, licences, registrations, certificates, accreditations and attestations (see "Using enhanced controls on the integrity of companies wishing to enter into contracts with public and municipal bodies" section in Chapter 4 for standards and approvals and the "Defining strategic contractual relationships with the private sector: a means of fighting corruption" section in Chapter 5 for AMP [Autorité des marches publics] authorisation). In addition to the eligibility conditions and in line with international best practice, Quebec has also introduced ineligibility conditions: a company that is found guilty of one of the offences set out in Annex I of the ACPB is ineligible for public contracts for a period of five years from the time that the guilty verdict is recorded in the register of companies ineligible for government contracts - RENA. These offences include acts of bribery, misrepresentation, fraud against the government and other instances of integrity violations. This register, which is kept by the President of the Treasury Board, can be consulted online: there were 764 companies were listed, 26% of which belong to the construction sector, as at 19/07/2018.

An objective assessment of a supplier's performance can identify irregularities in the performance of the contract and can be used as a warning system for integrity violations if this information is centralised. In Quebec, a best practice that is reflected in regulations and legislation is to use a supplier's poor performance evaluation to reserve the right to refuse participation in a tender process. For information technology contracts, government agencies must also record the supplier's positive or negative evaluation for contracts over USD 100 000 in a report. This provision is not included in all the ACPB's regulations, so the Government of Quebec would benefit from making it more widespread. In addition, as noted in the "Using a standardised environment to identify corruption risks during the contract performance phase" section in Chapter 5, this system is not centralised in the sense that a supplier's poor performance with one entity cannot be considered by a different public body in another procurement process. As stipulated in the Act to facilitate oversight of the contracts of public bodies and to establish the Public Procurement Authority– (Autorité des marchés publics, adopted on 1 December 2017), and in order to improve the system in place, the AMP's mandate is to centralise contractor performance evaluations so that public and municipal bodies can use them when evaluating bidders. However, for this provision to be effective, an implementing order must be adopted; the Government of Quebec would therefore benefit from implementing this system as quickly as possible in order to improve the efficiency and integrity of the system.

Award criteria that go beyond the price criterion

Recommendation No. 2 of the Charbonneau Commission promotes the use of award rules adapted to the nature of the works to be undertaken; the criteria for awarding contracts should therefore be carefully chosen to limit the risk of collusion and bribery but also to promote competition.

Promoting the use of multiple award criteria and incorporating the concept of the "most economically advantageous bid" in order to reduce the predictability of the bid

In Quebec, different rules apply depending on the subject matter of the contract. For example, in the case of contracts for professional services related to construction, public bodies are obliged to acquire the services of architects and engineers solely on the basis of the quality of the bid, since they are subject to mandatory tariffs set by the government.

In addition, for these organisations, the lowest compliant bidder rule generally applies. Although rules allowing the evaluation of the quality of the bid exist in some very specific cases, in practice it is the price criterion that is most frequently used. This elevates the risk of collusion and bribery since the main award criterion is predictable. The data provided by the TBS indicate that only 15% of the contracts of public bodies concluded between 2014 and 2017 include a quality criterion. Work is currently under way to propose new contractual rules and practices to public bodies to provide them with a wider range of tools to enable them to adapt their procurement strategy to the specific characteristics and particularities of each contract to be entered into (variable weighting of quality and price criteria).

For public and municipal bodies in Quebec, the regulatory framework allows for the evaluation of both price and quality. The concept of the most economically advantageous bid includes price, quality and other criteria that are not directly or separately taken into account by public bodies in Quebec, such as technical, aesthetic, environmental, social and technical assistance criteria, etc. Indeed, these criteria could in theory be considered under one of the "quality" sub-criteria. Moreover, by not grading technical aspects, public and municipal bodies do not encourage competition and innovation. The regulatory framework for municipal bodies further details the award criteria by providing for the use of "a system of weighting and evaluation of bids under which each bid is awarded a number of points based, in addition to price, on the quality or quantity of the goods, services or work, the terms of delivery, the maintenance services, the experience and financial capacity required of the insurer, supplier or contractor, or any other criteria directly related to the contract". The Government of Quebec could promote the use of multiple award criteria beyond price or total acquisition cost and quality, and could consider the possibility of integrating the notion of "most economically advantageous bid" into the regulatory framework to encourage greater competition and reduce the risk of predictability of calls for tender. In addition, guidelines on the use of the different criteria could be developed for all activity sectors to guide procurement officials in their choice of criteria.

Box 3.5. Award criteria for public procurement in the EU Procurement Directive

The Directive of the European Parliament and of the Council on public procurement (2014/24/EU) allows contracting authorities to take account of qualitative, environmental and social criteria when awarding a public contract. According to Article 67 of the Directive, public bodies shall base the award of public contracts on "*the most economically advantageous offer*". This shall be identified based on the price or cost, using a cost-effectiveness approach, assessed on the basis of criteria including qualitative, environmental and social aspects, linked to the subject-matter of the public contract in question.

Contracting authorities may thus consider the following criteria, with the tender documents specifying the relative weighting assigned to each of them:

1. **The quality** of the bid: the criteria may relate to technical merit, aesthetic and functional characteristics, accessibility, design for all users, social, environmental and innovative characteristics and trading and its conditions (Article 67 - 2a).
2. **The organisation, qualifications and experience of the staff** assigned to perform the contract: these criteria may be taken into account if they have a significant impact on the level of performance of the contract (Article 67 - 2b).
3. **The after-sales service, technical assistance and delivery conditions**, such as delivery date, delivery process and delivery period or period of completion (Article 67 - 2c).

Source: (European Commission, 2014[9]).

Considering the total acquisition cost criterion instead of the price criterion to ensure the true comparability of bids and establishing a Selection Committee when using the price criterion

When using the price criterion, care should be taken to ensure that the concept of total acquisition cost or life cycle costing (LCC) is used. This approach is being promoted in several countries, including countries subject to European Directives (Box 3.6 which provides Luxembourg as an example). Indeed, the integration of the different costs makes it possible to ensure better comparability of bids and limit the risk of integrity violations. In Quebec, despite the inclusion of this approach in certain regulations (Regulation respecting certain service contracts of public bodies – RCAOP, and the Regulation respecting contracting by public bodies in the field of information technologies – RCOPTI), its use remains very limited. The Government of Quebec could conduct awareness-raising and capacity-building activities to ensure greater dissemination and use of this concept. Officers responsible for enforcing contractual rules - RARCs could play an important role in promoting the use of the LCC.

Box 3.6. Total Life Cycle Costs in Luxembourg

In Luxembourg, Article 37 of the Law of 8 April 2018 on public procurement clearly defines the concept of Life Cycle Cost: it covers, insofar as they are relevant, all or some of the following costs of the life cycle of a product, service or work:

a. costs incurred by the contracting authority or other users, such as:
   - costs related to the acquisition
   - costs associated with use, such as the consumption of energy and other resources
   - maintenance costs
   - end-of-life costs such as collection and recycling costs.
b. costs attributed to environmental externalities associated with the product, service or facility during its life cycle, provided that their monetary value can be determined and verified.

Where contracting authorities assess costs according to a life-cycle costing method, they shall indicate in the tender documents the data to be provided by bidders and the method that the contracting authority will use to determine the life-cycle cost based on this data.

Source: (Government of the Grand Duchy of Luxembourg, 2018[10]).

For all tendering procedures that include a quality criterion, a selection committee meets to assess the quality of the various bids submitted. However, where the price criterion is used, there is no committee or other mechanism to ensure that decisions regarding the technical and administrative compliance of the bid are not taken by a single person. The Government of Quebec should therefore consider setting up a committee or another mechanism for tender procedures that include only the price criterion to evaluate the conformity of bids.

Greater transparency in the system of contract management in public procurement

Transparency is a key mechanism for strengthening the integrity of the public procurement system and for mitigating its inherent risks. This is a fundamental principle of the OECD Recommendation on Public Procurement and the OECD Recommendation on Public Integrity (OECD, 2015[1]; OECD, 2017[11]). Indeed, disclosure of information on contract management processes helps to identify and then mitigate mismanagement, fraud and bribery and helps to increase the accountability of contractors. Transparency also ensures the fair and equitable treatment of potential suppliers, while providing the necessary information to the general public. In Quebec, transparency is one of the principles that the regulatory framework for public procurement aims to promote. However, several recommendations of the Charbonneau Commission seek to further improve transparency in public procurement.

Improving transparency and information sharing throughout the contract management cycle

An efficient and integrated contract management system requires an adequate degree of transparency at all stages of the contract management cycle with all important and relevant information easily accessible to all stakeholders.

Publishing the entire regulatory framework for public procurement in Quebec on a single web page

The regulatory framework governing contract management for public bodies is published on the TBS site. It lists the various acts, regulations and orders covering public procurement in Quebec. Municipal legislation is published on the MAMH website, since the laws governing municipalities are the responsibility of the Minister of Municipal Affairs and Housing and not of the President of the Treasury Board. However, municipal laws are not accessible on the same page, although there is a link between the TBS site and the MAMH site. To ensure clarity of the regulatory framework, all statutory instruments should be listed and accessible from a single web page.

Providing more information on contract management, in particular for the upstream phase and the contract performance phase

The risks of integrity violations are present throughout the contract management cycle. Therefore, the publication of information about the contract management system and each procurement procedure allows for better monitoring of public expenditure by different stakeholders. In Quebec, a lot of documents and information are available on the SEAO. However, transparency could be improved in particular in the pre-tendering phase and during the performance of the contract.

Pre-tendering phase:

In terms of best practice, public entities should publish their procurement plans and issue information notices in advance, so that potential suppliers are aware of procurement opportunities and are better prepared to respond to CFTs, thus creating a more competitive environment and reducing the risk of integrity violations (OECD, 2018[12]). In Quebec, the documentation in the pre-tendering section is specific to each organisation. The SEAO provides companies with access to a website that offers value-added services in the construction field, including the dissemination of a preliminary draft, presenting a summary description of a project planned by a public body or a private company. However, this subscription only relates to the construction sector and is subject to a charge. The Government of Quebec should therefore consider requiring all public and municipal bodies to publish their procurement plans and, where relevant, to publish advance information notices and to allow free access in the new version of the SEAO to be implemented in 2022. In the meantime, the Quebec government could encourage public and municipal bodies to publish their procurement plans on their own websites. Box 3.7 describes the system in place in Australia.

Box 3.7. Publication of procurement plans in Australia

In Australia, government agencies are required to publish an Annual Procurement Plan under the Commonwealth Procurement Rules. This plan is published on the Australian Government's centralised procurement information system, AusTender, and must contain the following elements:

- A Strategic Procurement Outlook Statement outlining the agency's role and the main strategic goals for which it anticipates the use of public procurement.
- A brief description of the Planned Procurements for the coming year.

All plans are available on the AusTender website. They may be revised or cancelled, and do not constitute a call for tenders or a commitment to purchase the goods and services described.

Source: (OECD, 2016[2]).

In the case of direct awards, the publication of a notice of intent in the case of sole sourcing is mandatory for all bodies as of May 2019. Indeed, this provision is considered to be best practice as it ensures that there is some competition by allowing other suppliers to come forward and suspend the direct award procedure if necessary. However, for this strategy to be effective, suppliers that may be capable of challenging this procedure must be informed of its existence. An alert system, modelled on the existing one for CFT notices, would make it possible to provide this information to potential suppliers. As part of the development of new functionalities for the SEAO, it is therefore essential that the Government of Quebec pursue its objective of introducing such an alert system.

In addition, the notices published on the site come from ministries and public bodies, those in the health and social services network, organisations in the education network and Quebec municipalities, which also distribute their call for tender documents through the SEAO. However, state-owned enterprises are only required to publish CFT notices. The Government of Quebec should therefore consider making it mandatory for state-owned enterprises to use the SEAO for the publication of all notices and CFT documents.

Contract performance phase:

In Quebec, each public or municipal body has its own system for monitoring contract performance. Therefore, there is no real-time information sharing on the purchasing operations undertaken by public entities. As part of the ongoing work to define the needs of a new version of the SEAO to be implemented in 2022, the Government of Quebec could therefore consider developing an information system that provides open, shareable, reusable data on public procurement throughout the contract management cycle, starting with the planning stage for all organisations. This could reduce the risks of integrity violations and increase transparency and levels of citizen trust.

During this phase, there may be a discrepancy between the planned purchases, and those actually made in terms of expenses or deadlines. Governments therefore have to provide civil society, but also all stakeholders, with clear information on how taxpayer money is spent. Several initiatives aim to promote this type of standard, such as the "Open Contracting Standards" initiative. Indeed, many countries have implemented such standards to improve the accountability, transparency and integrity of their systems. This is the case of the "OpenCantieri" project set up for infrastructure projects in Italy (see Box 3.8).

Box 3.8. The "Open Cantieri" project in Italy

OpenCantieri is a project promoted and managed by the Ministry of Infrastructure and Transport (MIT) that presents open, comprehensive and up-to-date information on the process of building public infrastructure.

Data produced and published by public sources is integrated into a single platform with specific summaries and views. The information is fully accessible and can be downloaded from the MIT's Open Data page.

For each public infrastructure project, it is possible to access several pieces of information including:

1. the project implementation stage
2. the funding and the actual cost
3. any delays in implementation as well as any related explanations
4. the number of working days actually spent on this project.

Source: (Ministry of Infrastructure and Transport, Italy, 2018[13]).

Moreover, during this phase, the only obligation on public and municipal bodies is to publish any additional expenditure resulting from an amendment to the contract that exceeds the initial amount by more than 10% as well as the final amount paid at the end of the contract. However, price is not the only element that can be amended in a contract and that can impact on the competitive environment of a particular tender process. For example, a change in delivery times, or the quality of goods, services and public works can have a clear impact on the tendering environment. The regulatory framework emphasises that "a contract may be amended where the amendment is ancillary to the contract and does not change its nature", however, this analysis depends on an individual assessment and may not be applied consistently. To improve the transparency of the system and strengthen public confidence, it would therefore be appropriate for the Government of Quebec to publish all contract amendments.

Avoiding the use of public bid openings to reduce the risk of bid-rigging agreements between bidders

In Quebec, bid opening is made public. However, as stated in the OECD Recommendation on Fighting Bid Rigging, it's necessary to "Design the tender process so as to reduce the opportunities for communication among bidders either before or during the tender process" (OECD, 2012[8]). Indeed, direct communication between suppliers should be limited as much as possible in order to reduce the risks of collusion. The Government of Quebec should therefore consider ways to limit the use of public bid openings while putting in place mechanisms to ensure that this step is carried out properly. One such mechanism is to conduct contract management procedures electronically. This eliminates the need for a public bid opening (see "Towards greater digitalisation of the contract management system in the service of integrity" section).

Providing consolidated information and statistics on the entire contract management system in Quebec

Currently, information on the contract management system can be found mainly in the statistical report on contracts of public bodies. Similar information at municipal level does not exist. The Government of Quebec will therefore have to consider providing consolidated statistical data. In addition to descriptive information, it is important to include performance monitoring indicators for the contract management system in general, including indicators related to complaints. Several OECD countries provide detailed reports on the contract management system, e.g. Chile, where the annual report on the management of public accounts in relation to public procurement includes various figures and indicators, but also information on current developments in the system based on three strategic priorities: efficiency and competitiveness, probity and transparency, and access to procurement opportunities (ChileCompra, 2017[14]).

Towards greater digitalisation of the contract management system in the service of integrity

The use of digital technologies in the public sector is also a factor affecting efficiency which supports effective policy implementation and monitoring. Digitalisation increases transparency, facilitates access to public procurement and improves integrity by reducing the direct interaction between public procurement agents and businesses. It can also facilitate the detection of irregularities and corruption, such as manipulation of bid submissions (OECD, 2016[2]).

Integrating additional functionalities into the SEAO and providing clear deadlines for the mandatory use of electronic bid submission

In recognition of the benefits of e-procurement, countries are increasingly digitising their contract management processes, covering the entire contract management cycle. Figure 3.3 shows the main functionalities covered by these systems in some OECD countries.

Figure 3.3. Functionalities of e-procurement systems in OECD countries

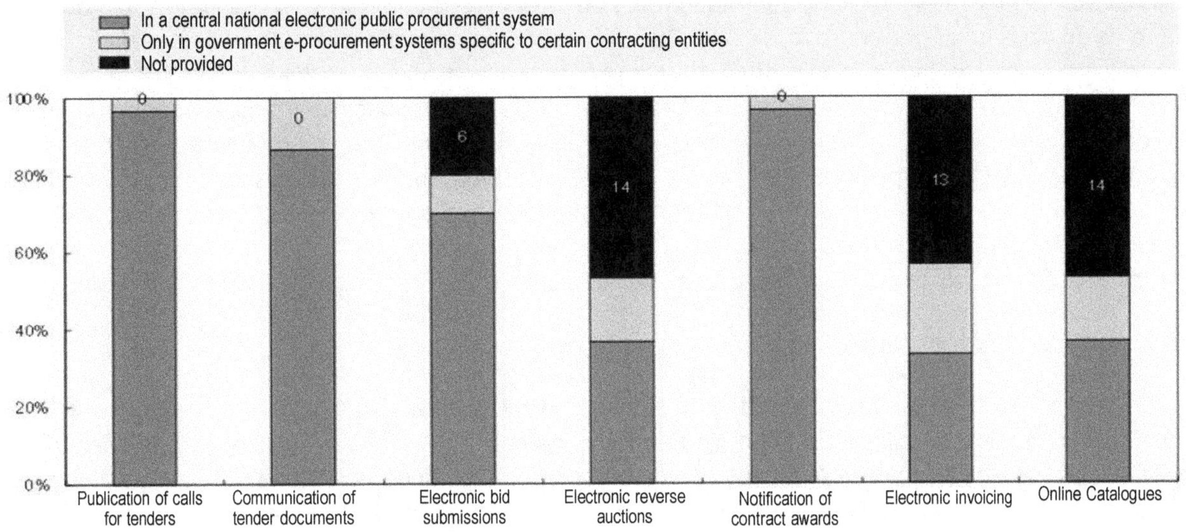

In a central national electronic public procurement system
Only in government e-procurement systems specific to certain contracting entities
Not provided

100%
80%
60%
40%
20%
0%

0 0 6 14 0 13 14

Publication of calls for tenders
Communication of tender documents
Electronic bid submissions
Electronic reverse auctions
Notification of contract awards
Electronic invoicing
Online Catalogues

Source: (OECD, 2017[15]).

In terms of functionalities, Quebec's electronic tendering system (the SEAO) seems to be used mainly as a platform for publishing notices and documents relating to public procurement. Indeed, the publication of CFT documents on the SEAO is mandatory for all public bodies, except for government enterprises (CFT notices only). The results of CFTs must also be published on a mandatory basis in the SEAO when this procedure is used.

Several subscription formulas are possible with monthly prices ranging from USD 6.65 to USD 119.95. The free formula allows consultation of certain documents and information only. The system does not yet have some of the key functionalities compliant with international best practices, in particular electronic reverse auctions, electronic catalogues and electronic invoicing. Given their advantages in terms of efficiency and integrity, the Government of Quebec should consider integrating these functionalities into future developments of the SEAO. Following Recommendation 1 of the Charbonneau Commission, responsibility for establishing the operating rules of the SEAO will be transferred to the Authority, who will work on this jointly with the TBS, six months after the CEO takes office.

A key functionality for improving integrity in the contract management system is the electronic submission of bids as it reduces contact between public officials and suppliers, improves the efficiency of the system, and increases competition. Quebec introduced this functionality on 18 June 2018, however current regulations do not require bidders and public bodies to use it. Moreover, no gradual approach is planned for the roll-out of electronic submission of bids. The Government of Quebec should provide clear deadlines for bidders to send their bids electronically for all tenders, regardless of the amount. For example, the European public procurement directives published in 2014 have set clear deadlines for the use of electronic tendering: from 1 April 2017 for central purchasing bodies and from 1 October 2018 for all other purchasers (European Commission, 2018[16]). The electronic submission of bids may also enable the Government of Quebec to centrally collect data on bidders and potential suppliers, to implement key performance indicators and identify certain warning signs related to collusion or bribery.

Developing an electronic system for expenditure below the minimum threshold

The publication of the results of any contract awards on the SEAO is currently only mandatory for contracts with a value equal to or greater than USD 25 000. Information on expenditure below this threshold is only available in the internal information system of each public/municipal body or in the estimates of expenditure in the National Assembly, which makes centralised use of this data impossible. To collect data and ensure the integrity of the system for these expenditures, the Government of Quebec could eventually develop a module in the SEAO or a specific electronic system. For example, countries such as Italy which have faced considerable challenges in terms of strengthening integrity, have set up an electronic market place for below-threshold purchases. (Box 3.9)

Box 3.9. The electronic market place for low-value public procurement in Italy: The MePa

Launched in 2003 and currently operating based on an electronic catalogue of over one million articles, the MePA online platform is one of the main electronic marketplaces currently used in Europe. Managed by Consip, the MePA provides a paperless environment for awarding public contracts for (mainly) low-value goods and services. The MePA seeks to encourage, in particular, the participation of SMEs in public procurement by offering operational flexibility and allowing direct award from standardised online catalogues and electronic auctions as a means of requesting quotations by, among other things:

1. free registration for suppliers and buyers
2. digitised transactions
3. use of electronic signatures to ensure compliance and transparency
4. providing an open platform for the publication of standardised online catalogues.

Source: (EBRD, European Bank for Reconstruction and Development), 2017.

Developing a supplier database

In a contract management system, it is important to have a supplier database to provide all organisations with access to a larger number of potential suppliers and limit the risk of integrity violations. For private companies, registration in the database can help them avoid having to provide administrative documents for each bid submission. There is no supplier database in Quebec, while at the federal government level, one does exist. The Government of Quebec could therefore consider developing such a database. Indeed, the development of such a database would also be very useful for ITT and direct awards in order to identify more suppliers. For example, South Korea has an electronic public procurement system called KONEPS. This system has a supplier database that public entities can use to search for potential suppliers; it also means that companies do not need to send administrative documents for each new submission once they have registered in the system (PPS, 2014[17]). In France, a similar system has also been put in place via the “tell us once” principle: any information on suppliers that is already held by a French administrative body will no longer have to be requested from participants as part of an electronic bid (Ministry of Economy and Finance, France, 2017[18]).

Action plan

Public Procurement methods

- Promoting competitive procedures below the thresholds by introducing an intermediate threshold above which entities must use the ITT
- Providing clear rules and guidelines for the use of all exceptions, particularly for the concepts of "confidentiality and protected information"
- Promoting more competition for CFT exceptions
- Harmonising exceptions to CFTs between the regulatory frameworks for public and municipal bodies
- Making a clear distinction between exceptions to CFTs and those falling under exclusions and exemptions from the regulatory framework for public procurement
- Continuing efforts to enhance controls over the use of exceptions to competitive procedures

Selection and award criteria

- Centralising publication of information on supplier performance
- Promoting the use of multiple award criteria and incorporating the concept of the "most economically advantageous bid" to reduce the predictability of the bid
- Considering the total acquisition cost criterion instead of the price criterion to ensure a true comparability of bids, and establishing a Selection Committee when using the price criterion

Transparency

- Publishing the entire regulatory framework for public procurement in Quebec on a single web page
- Providing more information on contract management, in particular for the upstream phase and the contract performance phase
- Avoiding the use of public bid openings to reduce the risk of bid-rigging agreements between bidders
- Providing consolidated information and statistics on the entire contract management system in Quebec
- Integrating additional functionalities into the SEAO and providing clear deadlines for the mandatory use of electronic bid submission
- Developing an electronic system for expenditure below the minimum threshold
- Developing a supplier database

References

ChileCompra (2017), "Cuenta Publica - Gestion 2017", http://www.mercadopublico.cl (accessed on 23 July 2018). [14]

Crown Commercial Service (2017), *General Legal Advice Services*, https://ccs-agreements.cabinetoffice.gov.uk/contracts/rm3786 (accessed on 18 July 2018). [6]

European Commission (2018), *E-procurement*, https://ec.europa.eu/growth/single-market/public-procurement/digital_en (accessed on 23 July 2018). [16]

European Commission (2014), *Directive 2014/24/UE du Parlement européen et du Conseil du 26 février 2014 sur la passation des marchés publics et abrogeant la directive 2004/18/CE*, http://data.europa.eu/eli/dir/2014/24/oj. [9]

Government of France (2019), *Code de la commande publique*, Direction des Affaires Juridiques, https://www.legifrance.gouv.fr/affichCode.do?cidTexte=LEGITEXT000037701019&dateTexte=20190524 (accessed on 25 July 2018). [7]

Government of the Grand Duchy of Luxembourg (2018), *Loi du 8 avril 2018 sur les marchés publics*, http://marches.public.lu/fr/legislation/marches-publics.html (accessed on 25 July 2018). [10]

Ministry of Economy and Finance, France (2017), "Transformation numérique de la commande publique 2017-2022", https://www.economie.gouv.fr/files/files/directions_services/daj/marches_publics/dematerialisation/plan-transform-numeriq-cp/Feuillet_Plan-Transfo-Num-CP.pdf (accessed on 23 July 2018). [18]

Ministry of Infrastructure and Transport, Italy (2018), *OpenCantieri*, http://opencantieri.mit.gov.it/ (accessed on 26 July 2018). [13]

OECD (2019), *Enhancing the Use of Competitive Tendering in Costa Rica's Public Procurement System: Streamlining the exceptions and redesigning the threshold system*, OECD, Paris, https://www.oecd.org/countries/costarica/costa-rica-public-procurement-system.pdf. [3]

OECD (2018), *Procurement Review of the Chamber of Commerce of Bogotá, Colombia: Aligning practices with the OECD Public Procurement Recommendation*, OECD, Paris, http://www.oecd.org/gov/public-procurement/publications/procurement-review-chamber-commerce-bogota.pdf. [12]

OECD (2017), *Government at a Glance 2017*, OECD Publishing, Paris, https://dx.doi.org/10.1787/gov_glance-2017-en. [15]

OECD (2017), *OECD Recommendation of the Council on Public Integrity*, OECD, Paris, http://www.oecd.org/gov/ethics/OECD-Recommendation-Public-Integrity.pdf. [11]

OECD (2016), *Preventing Corruption in Public Procurement*, OECD, Paris, http://www.oecd.org/gov/public-procurement/publications/Corruption-Public-Procurement-Brochure.pdf. [2]

OECD (2015), *OECD Recommendation of the Council on Public Procurement*, OECD, Paris, https://www.oecd.org/gov/public-procurement/OECD-Recommendation-on-Public-Procurement.pdf. [1]

OECD (2012), *OECD Recommendation of the Council on Fighting Bid Rigging in Public Procurement*, OECD, Paris, https://www.oecd.org/daf/competition/RecommendationOnFightingBidRigging2012.pdf. [8]

Office of Government Procurement (2017), *Public Procurement Guidelines for Goods and Services*, https://ogp.gov.ie/public-procurement-guidelines-for-goods-and-services/ (accessed on 18 July 2018). [5]

PPS (2014), *"What is integrated Korea ON-line E-Procurement System (KONEPS)?"*, Public Procurement Service, https://www.pps.go.kr/eng/jsp/koneps/overview.eng (accessed on 23 July 2018). [17]

Treasury Board Secretariat (2017), "Statistiques sur les contrats des organismes publics 2016-2017", https://www.tresor.gouv.qc.ca/fileadmin/PDF/faire_affaire_avec_etat/statistiques/1617.pdf (accessed on 18 July 2018). [4]

4 Business integrity and competition among public procurement suppliers in Quebec

This chapter examines the steps taken by Quebec to strengthen the integrity of suppliers in public procurement, as well as measures to ensure that bidding deadlines and regulatory constraints do not undermine competition among suppliers. First, the chapter analyses the controls in place to limit undue influence in communications with the private sector at the market analysis stage. This chapter also explores the enforcement of the contract authorisation regime in certain public procurement contracts and its impact on the adoption of good governance and control measures by suppliers. Finally, the chapter addresses the matter of bidding deadlines, which are shorter in Quebec than in other jurisdictions, and regulatory requirements (approvals, certifications of compliance with technical standards), which sometimes lead to increased risks of collusion and bribery due to weak competition.

Communicating with the private sector and strengthening business integrity

The Government of Quebec has made significant efforts in recent years to strengthen business integrity and reduce the undue influence exercised by businesses in the conduct of public procurement. However, these efforts should not be made at the expense of efficient procurement, sound communication with potential bidders, and competition in the conduct of public procurement.

Fostering effective communication with the private sector while reducing the risk of collusion and bribery

To reduce opportunities for bribery and collusion in public procurement processes, several OECD member countries limit direct contacts between public procurement officials and suppliers. Public procurement processes are disseminated through an internet platform through which suppliers can obtain tender documents and submit their bids. The use of these platforms also provides a means of communicating fairly and transparently with potential suppliers in order to, for example, conduct a market analysis before organising the call for tenders.

Maximising the potential of the SEAO for fair and transparent communication with suppliers

In 2011, the regulations on contracts for public and municipal bodies were amended so that tender documents and related addenda are distributed exclusively through the electronic tendering system (SEAO). One of the aims of this measure was to combat collusion and malpractice in public procurement more effectively by avoiding direct contacts between potential bidders, as well as between potential bidders and public procurement officials.

With the advent of this requirement, public and municipal bodies no longer communicate directly with bidders prior to the determination of the winning tender. The purpose of this practice is to avoid giving a company an advantage over its competitors by providing it with insider information. In order to notify potential bidders that a call for tenders has been issued, potential bidders may receive a notification from the SEAO that a call for tender (CFT) has been issued in their area. Public and municipal bodies can also use the SEAO to conduct a call for interest, which allows them to survey the market to find out if there is a product or service to meet a specific need, as well as to issue a notice of intent, which ensures that no other potential contractor can provide an item or service below the public call for tenders threshold. The use of calls for interest and notices of intent are currently not supervised and are little used in practice. However, the use of notices of intent will become mandatory for all direct awards above the CFT threshold on an exceptional basis, where the public body believes it can demonstrate that a call for tenders would not be in the public interest. As part of future developments of the platform, and as noted in Chapter 3, registered suppliers will receive these notices of intent by default, unless they have voluntarily changed their profile settings to not receive them.

The Government of Quebec has put in place targeted communications to obtain feedback on its public procurement processes and to make bidders aware of its ethical and lobbying standards. The Government of Quebec requires contracting authorities to include in their tender documents a questionnaire to find out the reasons why a company did not submit a bid, even though it had obtained the tender documents. In addition, the tender documents outline the rules to be followed under the *Lobbying Transparency and Ethics Act* and the *Lobbyists' Code of Conduct*. Each bid must include a statement that the communications between the public body and the bidder, if any, were made in accordance with the Act and the Code. Some contracting authorities also communicate with unsuccessful bidders upon request in order to help them improve their future bids, and encourage them to participate in future calls for tenders. Finally, the MTQ organises biannual round tables to obtain feedback from construction and engineering firms on the conduct of the ministry's public procurement.

Communicating with bidders through a web-based platform such as the SEAO is best practice in line with trends in other OECD member countries (OECD, 2016[1]). Procurement units must exercise great care to communicate fairly and transparently with suppliers to ensure that competition is not unduly distorted. Thus, meetings should be prepared and structured to produce maximum results (Box 4.1) while avoiding the disclosure of strategic information that could facilitate bid-rigging agreements (price evaluation, volumes, etc.). Procurement units can also prepare a template to record and communicate the results of the supplier meetings via the web platform. The results of the meetings may also be used to purchase similar goods, services or work in the future.

Box 4.1. Proposals for structuring information meetings with suppliers

Some questions to bear in mind when meeting with suppliers:

- Are you interested in this opportunity? If not, why not?
- Is the economic model realistic?
- Are the business objectives realistic? Are the business opportunities interesting?
- In your opinion, what are the main risks?
- Can you give an idea of the costs, their main determinants and how they can be minimised?
- Can you give a general indication of the likely time frame for preparation and implementation?
- Are there other, more effective approaches?
- What added value can the supplier bring?
- Are there examples of good or bad practice in how other organisations have tried to obtain the same products or services, and what can be done to ensure clarity and improve results?

It is useful to meet with different types of suppliers to bolster policy options; for example, the views of small and medium-sized enterprises (SMEs) may be different from those of large corporations.

Public procurement officials should be present at meetings with suppliers, while on the supplier side, it should be someone with a good understanding of the requirements, who can offer innovative solutions and constructive advice. Both parties should adopt an attitude favouring confidentiality, flexibility and openness.

The objective is to identify procurement risks and expected results. Communicating and meeting with suppliers also allows them to present their views on how the results could be achieved, their perception of the issues, and the timelines, feasibility and affordability of the project.

The results of these meetings help to define requirements that are in line with what the market can provide. The market may also be encouraged to move in certain directions that will allow these requirements to be met in the future.

Source: Based on presentations by Steve Graham, Hadley Graham Ltd, advisers to the United Kingdom Department of Health, at the OECD workshop on "Improving ISSSTE Public Procurement Practices", Mexico City, 2-4 September 2014.

Several OECD countries have adopted measures to provide a framework for transparent communications and consultations with suppliers, to level the playing field for all businesses, and to mitigate the risk of inappropriate relationships between government officials and suppliers (Box 4.2). For example, although Chile is often described as the country least affected by corruption in South America, public procurement is still a moderate risk there. Thus, the *ChileCompra* platform has been designed to mitigate the risk of wrongdoings and undue influence as much as possible.

Box 4.2. Dialogue with suppliers: best international practice

"Welcome to Open Dialogue" in the United States

In 2014, the Chief Acquisition Officers Council (CAOC) created an online platform for stakeholders to discuss issues, barriers and possible solutions related to the federal acquisition process. The objective of the discussions is to identify improvements to the procurement cycle and the management of public procurement, and is part of an effort to improve the efficiency of the federal procurement system.

The dialogue focuses on three main areas: (i) reporting obligations and compliance requirements; (ii) public procurement practices; and (iii) participation of small businesses, new entrants and non-traditional government subcontractors. On the online platform, interested parties submit ideas, answer questions posed by the moderators and comment on other suggestions.

Online consultation of suppliers by the ChileCompra central purchasing department

Before issuing a call for tenders, ChileCompra *(Dirección de Compras y Contratación Pública*) engages in an open consultation of suppliers, which it announces online via its website www.mercadopublico.cl. The purpose of the consultation is to obtain information on prices, the characteristics of the goods and services desired, the time needed by suppliers to prepare their bids, and any other information that could contribute to the efficiency of the tendering process.

Following online publication of a contract notice (call for tenders), ChileCompra organises round tables with suppliers, also announced on its website. The purpose of these meetings is to inform suppliers of the main objectives of the procurement and to guide them on how to submit a bid. To enhance transparency, meetings are recorded and published online as a file attached to the call for tenders, so that suppliers who were unable to attend can also benefit from the information.

ChileCompra also has an online forum with a question and answer system for each call for tenders, which is set up before the deadline for the submission of bids. This forum is particularly useful for suppliers who are geographically distant from the capital Santiago (where Chile Compra's offices are located) and require remote access to the Q&A function, thus supporting transparency, fair treatment and free competition.

Relationship management in the evaluation of calls for tenders in Australia

The Government of South Australia's Department of Planning, Transport and Infrastructure (DPTI) has developed a Procurement Management Framework to address potential and significant conflicts of interest in public procurement and to mitigate the risk of inappropriate relationships between public officers and suppliers. Under this policy, DPTI members must immediately report any conflict of interest with a bidding company to the chair of the evaluation panel, including:

1. close family member employed by a bidding company
2. a relative participating in the company's bid preparation
3. regular contact with an employee of a bidding company
4. having received gifts, invitations or other similar benefits from a candidate company during the period prior to the launch of the call for tenders
5. having recently left a candidate company
6. being interested in a future job offer or other favours from a bidding company.

Sources: Chief Acquisition Officers Council (2014), http://exo.dialogue.cao.gov/; Presentations by Marjorie Ramírez, former head of the Framework Agreements Division of ChileCompra, at the OECD workshop on "Improving ISSSTE's Public Procurement Practices", Mexico City, 2-4 September 2014; Government of South Australia, "DPTI Procurement Practices and Policies", www.dpti.sa.gov.au/open_government/proactive_disclosure/details_of_procurement_practices_within_departments.

The Government of Quebec could therefore draw inspiration from the operation of these platforms in order to maximise the potential use of the SEAO. The SEAO could be used to publish notices of intent to call for tenders on a more systematic basis as appropriate, as well as meetings with suppliers as part of its market oversight approach. The online exchange forum function could also be used to strengthen communications with suppliers in a fair and transparent manner.

Developing tools to guide interaction with suppliers appropriately during the market research and knowledge acquisition phase

According to best practices in OECD countries, communication with suppliers is increasingly part of a market oversight and analysis approach. These functions are usually assigned upstream, to a sector technical expert, while procurement professionals work with the sector expert downstream in developing the procurement strategy and overseeing the procurement process. For example, the market analysis process of the Italian public procurement agency *Consip SpA* provides for well-coordinated dialogue with suppliers when the circumstances of a particular contract justify it (Box 4.3). This enhanced framework stems from the increased powers delegated to the Italian Anti-Corruption Agency (ANAC) following numerous cases of corruption in public procurement exposed by the Italian media.

Box 4.3. Market analysis process of the Italian central purchasing body, Consip SpA

Consip SpA, the Italian central purchasing agency, is fully owned by the Ministry of Economy and Finance. Consip is responsible for awarding contracts (usually framework agreements) for goods and services for the Italian public sector.

To improve its purchases, Consip has developed an internal procedure on how to conduct a market analysis and how to interact with suppliers (economic operators) during market analysis.

The procedure, described in figure 4.1, identifies the actions to be performed during the market analysis to finalise a "feasibility study", a stage prior to the design of the call for tenders and the publication of the tender notice.

The entire process is supported by: 1) internal guidelines on market analysis; 2) market consultation questionnaires; and 3) a yearly Sourcing Activities Plan (SAP).

Figure 4.1. Market analysis process of the Italian central purchasing body, Consip SpA

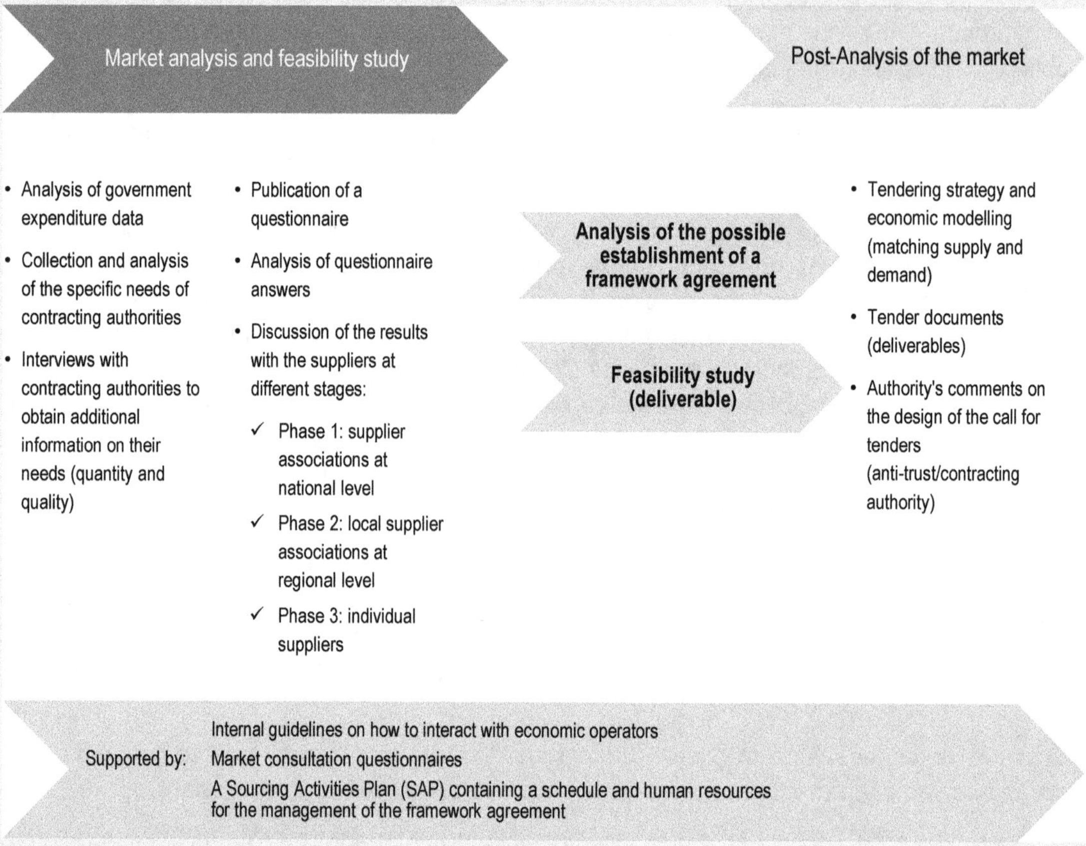

Internal guidelines on market analysis

The internal guidelines on market analysis are intended to guide the interaction with companies during the market consultation phase. The purpose of the market analysis is to collect the following data on the characteristics of the goods and services required:

- market size and volume of purchases in relation to market size
- market structure: percentage of small and medium-sized enterprises in this market segment or dominance of large companies
- main suppliers on the market
- maturity of products/services, pricing models and conditions offered by suppliers, potential standardisation of products/services and business capabilities
- prospects for market development in the coming years.

This information is useful for defining the procurement characteristics, the tendering strategy, the possibility of sub-division into batches and the reference price.

Information is collected through meetings held with the main professional associations and, where necessary, with individual suppliers, following the guidelines for market analysis.

Market consultation questionnaires and meetings with economic operators

The market consultation begins with the publication of project-specific questionnaires on the e-procurement platform and the Consip website. The questionnaires provided to suppliers aim to gain a better understanding of the characteristics of the market, to guarantee the participation of companies and to ensure the dissemination of information. The questionnaires are valid until the publication of the call for tenders notice.

Meetings with economic operators may take place; these must be requested by e-mail and at least two Consip employees (project leader and category manager) must attend. During the meeting, Consip presents the project-specific market research questionnaire and distributes a copy of its code of ethics. The questionnaire is then completed by all those attending the meeting.

Questions may be asked during the meeting; however, no information beyond what is already published is provided, so that suppliers who are unable to attend the meeting are not disadvantaged. The tendering strategy (if already established) is not discussed and no comparison between potential bidders is made.

Source: Consip SpA.

In Quebec, the Directive Concerning the Management of the Supply, Service and Construction Contracts of Public Bodies provides a framework for communications of influence in public procurement. However, the Directive does not provide any guidelines or standards of conduct for situations where officials wish to acquire specific information on specific contracts. The CSPQ has also developed the guide *Reference Process in Contractual Management of Supply and Service Contracts*, which provides a comprehensive general reference framework for contract management. Nevertheless, this guide provides limited guidance on the suitability and methodologies for approaching key actors in specific markets.

To enhance its understanding of the capacity of markets to meet its needs, the Government of Quebec could make tools available to public and municipal bodies to conduct market analysis and monitoring activities, including the oversight of exchanges with potential bidders when warranted by circumstances. Box 4.3 provides concrete examples of tools that the Government of Quebec could use to achieve this. In addition, the AMP, as part of its monitoring and recommendation remit, may also suggest specific practices that it deems appropriate based on its findings in the exercise of its activities.

Using enhanced controls on the integrity of companies wishing to enter into contracts with public and municipal bodies

In response to the many cases of collusion and bribery brought before the Charbonneau Commission, the Government of Quebec has implemented innovative and ambitious measures to strengthen business integrity in Quebec. On 7 December 2012, the ACPB was amended to introduce the contract authorisation regime, which involves verifying the integrity of companies wishing to enter into a contract with a public body covered by the ACPB or a municipal body. The arrangement also applies to all subcontractors taking part in a public contract as soon as the value of the subcontract is greater than or equal to the applicable threshold. The United States has also adopted a system of corporate control that includes: 1) a centralised list of companies authorised to contract with the state; and 2) a list of companies that cannot receive federal contracts. However, this control system is not as thorough as in Quebec because it does not include in-company audits such as those conducted by the UPAC (Box 4.4).

Box 4.4. The system for managing the award of public procurement contracts in the United States

In the United States, the System for Award Management (SAM) is a single interface created in 2012 and operated by the federal government. It brings together several databases previously used in public procurement, including a mandatory registration system (Central Contractor Registration) and a list of suppliers debarred from all procurement processes (Excluded Parties List System).

To be eligible to enter into public procurement contracts with the Federal Government, suppliers are required to register in the SAM and to update their data once a year. The information to be provided includes general information (company address, unique identification number) as well as tax and banking data. If the registration was made with the help of a US Federal Contractor Registration case manager, companies receive a Verified Vendor Seal indicating that their information has been verified, thus avoiding any risk of error or omission. This certification can be posted on a company's website provided that the link to the certification document is included.

In addition, a company may be suspended or debarred from participation in a procurement process by a federal agency in the event of certain failures specified in the Federal Acquisition Regulation. Examples of such failures include bribery, breach of a previous contract or any offence indicating a lack of integrity. The list of suppliers who are not eligible to receive federal contracts or sub-contracts is available on the SAM website.

Sources: US Federal Contractor Registration, https://uscontractorregistration.com/; Federal Acquisition Regulation https://www.acquisition.gov/browsefar.

To be eligible to enter into a contract with a public or municipal body, the company must obtain a contract authorisation from the AMP following a review of the integrity of the company, its shareholders, partners, directors or leaders, or a person or entity that has, directly or indirectly, legal or de facto control over it (the management of the contract authorisation regime has been transferred from the *Autorité des marchés financiers* to the AMP, which has held the responsibility for it since January 2019). This integrity review is conducted by the Anti-Corruption Associate Commissioner, within the UPAC, which is mandated to carry out the necessary checks and provide the AMP with all the relevant information when deciding to issue the authorisation.

Defining targets with specific indicators for the exercise of discretionary power under the contract authorisation regime

The ACPB gives broad discretion to the AMP to demand corrective measures from companies wishing to obtain authorisation to enter into contracts with public bodies but that do not meet the high standards of integrity that the public has a right to expect from a party to a public contract, as defined in articles 21.27 and 21.28 of the ACPB. The establishment of clear and transparent objectives for the contract authorisation regime could make it possible to measure its performance against predetermined objectives, thus allowing for the adjustment of the benchmarks for the exercise of discretionary power if necessary.

Setting clear and measurable objectives for the contract authorisation regime

Companies whose integrity is not in doubt receive their contract authorisation within five to ten months without any particular requirements. However, the ACPB requires that the AMP refuse to issue a contract authorisation if the company's majority shareholder, (where this is an individual), or a director or CEO of the company, has been convicted of an offence under annex I of the ACPB within the last five years.

Additionally, the ACPB states that the AMP may refuse to grant (or may revoke) a contract authorisation to a company that does not meet "the high standards of integrity that the public has a right to expect of a party to a public contract". As stated in the report of the Quebec Auditor General (QAG), "integrity is in itself a concept that can be highly subjective" and in this sense, "the legislator has granted very broad discretionary powers" to the AMP. The ACPB also provides a framework for dealing with what constitutes a lack of integrity on the part of companies. For example, it includes the following:

- ties to a criminal organisation;
- the fact that the company or any of its directors, CEOs or shareholders have been prosecuted for one of the offences listed in annex I of the ACPB, or any other offence of a criminal nature;
- the fact that the company or one of its directors, CEOs or shareholders has repeatedly evaded or attempted to evade the law;
- the fact that the company requesting the authorisation is a front for, or the successor to, an undertaking that would not receive authorisation.

This power of intervention of the UPAC and the AMP is generally broader than similar powers of intervention in other jurisdictions (Box 4.5).

Box 4.5. Debarment from public procurement procedures for violations of integrity

Violations of integrity committed by certain companies may lead to the temporary or permanent debarment of a bidder from participation in a public procurement procedure. The 2009 OECD Recommendation which aims to strengthen the fight against corruption calls on the Parties to the Convention on Combating Bribery of Foreign Public Officials in International Business Transactions to "*suspend, to an appropriate degree, from competition for public contracts or other public advantages (...) enterprises determined to have bribed domestic public officials*".

The adoption of bidder debarment systems has increased significantly over the last decade, both as an instrument for fighting corruption and as a tool for restoring confidence in public procurement. Several countries and multilateral organisations have developed such systems, but their operation differs from jurisdiction to jurisdiction. In addition, there are wide variations in the grounds for debarment (Hjelmeng and Søreide, 2014), and some countries are reviewing their debarment processes to reduce their rigidity.

European Union

Following the European Union (EU) legislation, there are mandatory debarment rules in EU Member States. According to Article 57 of Directive 2014/24/EU of 26 February 2014 on the award of public contracts, contracting authorities are obliged to exclude an economic operator from participation in a public procurement procedure where the operator has been convicted on the following grounds:

- Participation in a criminal organisation;
- Bribery;
- Fraud;
- Terrorist offence or offence related to terrorist activities;
- Money laundering or terrorist financing;
- Child labour and other forms of human trafficking.

In addition, economic operators must provide contracting authorities with a European Single Procurement Document (ESPD) certifying on their honour that they are not in a situation that could lead to their debarment (Article 59). The contracting authorities may require the production of certificates, declarations and other evidence of the absence of such grounds (Article 60).

Mexico

In Mexico, the Law on Public Sector Procurement, Leasing and Services *(Ley de Adquisiciones, Arrendamientos y Servicios del Sector Público*, LAASSP) includes various provisions on administrative sanctions for bidders and suppliers who have not complied with their contractual obligations (Articles 59 to 64 of the LAASSP). Penalties can range from a fine *(multas)* to debarment from public procurement procedures for a period from three months to five years *(inhabilitaciones)*. The list of suppliers that have been sanctioned or debarred at least once is published online. It specifies the reasons for the sanction or debarment, the amount of the fine and the duration of the exclusion. In October 2016, 1 236 suppliers were listed as having been sanctioned or debarred.

The entry into force of the Federal Act on Administrative Responsibilities *(Ley general de responsabilidades administrativas*, LGRA) in July 2017 enriched the legislative framework for public procurement. Unlike the Federal Law on the Administrative Responsibilities of Public Servants *(Ley Federal de Responsabilidades Administrativas de los Servidores Públicos*, LFRASP), which it replaced, the LGRA also applies to suppliers and bidders. Article 81 provides for sanctions against companies involved in public sector activities who are found guilty of serious administrative misconduct. These are listed in articles 65 to 72 of the law and include collusion, influence peddling and bribery of public officials. Companies may be prohibited from participating in acquisitions, leases, services or public works for a period of three months to ten years.

Multilateral Development Banks

Under the leadership of the World Bank, the Multilateral Development Banks developed and signed an Agreement for Mutual Enforcement of Debarment Decisions in April 2010 and publicised the list of companies and individuals ineligible to participate in their tendering process. Participating institutions must enforce decisions taken by anyone institution based on the four principles which they unanimously consider to justify sanctions: i) fraud; ii) corruption; iii) coercion; and iv) collusion.

Sources: (Hjelmeng and Søreide, 2014[2]; European Commission, 2014[3]; OECD, 2017[4]).
Agreement for Mutual Enforcement of Debarment Decisions, https://www.adb.org/sites/default/files/institutional-document/32774/files/cross-debarment-agreement.pdf

Given the potential impact of the contract authorisation regime on businesses and in order to exercise its broad discretion in a fair and consistent manner, the AMP has developed a number of benchmarks to ensure that its decisions are consistent with established precedents. Indeed, the AMP has broad powers to compel companies that have committed certain integrity failures (as defined by the AMP), to adopt governance and control measures that can reduce the risk of bribery in the conduct of public procurement. For example, the AMP may issue a demand for corrective action, requiring a company to put in place the necessary measures to ensure that integrity issues do not recur. The AMP may also issue a notice of refusal, which may or may not be maintained following the AMP's observations of the company's commitment to put certain corrective measures in place. If the notice of refusal is maintained, the company is entered in the register of ineligible companies (RENA) provided for in the ACPB for a period of five years. Companies are also listed in the RENA if they, or any person related [1]to them, are convicted of an offence identified in annex I of the ACPB.

The contract authorisation regime has had a positive impact on corporate governance. For example, more competition has been noted among engineering firms, as stated by the former Inspector General of the City of Montréal and the CEO of the *Association des firmes de génie-conseil du Québec* (Champagne, 2018[5]). While increased perceptions of greater competition among engineering firms is a positive development, further analysis is needed to gain a full picture of its impact on public procurement.

Nevertheless, following a report of the Auditor General of Quebec that questioned the consistency and appropriateness of the requirements demanded from certain companies that had received a request to implement corrective measures (VGQ, 2018[6]), the AMF is currently developing an action plan to put in place mechanisms to ensure the relevance and consistency across proposed measures. Beyond the establishment of enhanced institutional mechanisms for control of the requirements imposed, the AMP could set specific and measurable objectives that the authorisation regime aims to achieve. Prior identification of specific objectives could greatly facilitate the identification and application of solutions to each problematic situation within a company, thus ensuring greater consistency and objectivity. As an indication, Table 4.1 includes examples of objectives, monitoring measures and impact indicators that could be set in advance by the AMP to assess the performance of the contract authorisation regime.

Table 4.1. Examples of objectives, monitoring measures and impact indicators that could be established by the AMP

Examples of objectives	Examples of implementation monitoring measures	Examples of impact indicators
Preventing small companies where the natural person that is the majority shareholder has committed serious and repeated tax offences from obtaining publicly funded contracts	• Requiring a plan for the sale of the shareholder's shares to a natural or legal person unrelated to the shareholder • Requesting documentation certifying the sale of the shares and the identity of the new owner	• Number of enterprises with a natural person having committed serious and repetitive tax offences as a majority shareholder with a contract authorisation • Number of cases where the sale of shares to an unrelated person was successfully completed and the authorisation maintained • Number of cases where the authorisation was withdrawn
Preventing businesses linked to organised crime or guilty of offences included in annex I of the ACPB from reappearing in another legal form	• Not allowing the business to be transferred to or employ a natural or legal person related to a person with links to organised crime • Not issuing authorisations to companies with no assets or employees • Requiring disclosure of significant transfers of assets or employees within a specified period of time prior to the request for authorisation, or at any time during the term of the authorisation	• Identity of shareholders, leaders, directors or employees of an authorised business that has been transferred as a result of links to organised crime • Number of authorisations denied to companies with no assets or employees • Number and nature of significant reported transfers of assets or employees • Number of detected cases with significant unreported transfers of assets and employees
Ensuring that the contract authorisation procedure is adapted to the particularities of public procurement contracts	• Assessing the volume of contract authorisations issued for public procurement awards • Defining the types of companies holding the contract authorisations	• Ratio of public procurement contracts with a contract authorisation to total number of public procurement contracts awarded • Ratio of companies holding contract authorisation by type of procurement (professional services or construction) to the total number of companies for these types of procurement
Ascertaining the impact of the contract authorisation procedure on access to public procurement	• Assessing the efficiency of the contract authorisation procedure	• Average time taken to obtain a contract authorisation • Average number of public procurement contracts awarded to companies with a contract authorisation

Source: Work of the OECD, 2018.

These targets could be published to ensure natural justice for companies, which would further strengthen the incentives for companies to demonstrate good governance and integrity in the conduct of their business. Publication of the objectives would also increase transparency and accountability in the administration of the contract authorisation regime, including the AMP's interpretation of the term "high standards of integrity that the public has a right to expect from a party to a public contract or public sub-contract" included in the ACPB.

Prioritising controls on riskier public procurement contracts

Under article 21.17.1 of the ACPB, the government has broad discretionary powers to determine which contracts will be subject to the contract authorisation regime of the ACPB. The TBS could use this authority in the enforcement of the contract authorisation to target contracts that are at higher risk.

Considering extending the contract authorisation regime to more public contracts based on a risk analysis

The scope of the contract authorisation regime is currently limited to construction contracts over USD 5 million and service contracts over USD 1 million. This may exclude several high-risk markets from the scope of the contract authorisation regime.

It is understandable that a certain amount of restraint is exercised in defining the scope of the contract authorisation regime. As of July 2018, before the enforcement of the contract authorisation regime was transferred to the AMP, the AMF had received 5 478 requests for authorisation under these thresholds, and if the government decided to follow through on its commitment to lower the threshold for all government contracts to USD 100 000, approximately 20 000 companies would have to apply for contract authorisation. According to the information provided by the AMF, the time taken to obtain an authorisation can vary from 5 to 10 months based on the best case scenario, or even longer in cases where major issues are detected. Thus, the scope of the contract authorisation regime should be extended by the Government of Quebec only on a well-considered basis, taking account of internal capacities to safeguard procurement efficiency.

That being said, the government may consider using its discretion under article 21.17.1 of the ACPB to subject certain additional public procurement contracts to the contract authorisation regime based on risk analysis, audit results and the strategic importance of certain stakeholders to ensure the integrity of public procurement. For example, few construction site oversight contracts require authorisation given the USD 1 million threshold. In addition, for technical reasons, procurement sub-contracts within public construction contracts are not subject to contract authorisation because the regulations do not recognise them as public sub-contracts. However, there are several documented cases where the supply of raw materials for major construction sites is embezzled, replaced with inferior materials, and overestimated in terms of volumes delivered (PwC, 2014[7]). The supply of computer equipment through the Shared Services Centre of Québec has also been identified as a risk area by the QAG (VGQ, 2016[8]).

Nevertheless, any such decisions to extend the scope of the regime should be taken in the light of the capacity to analyse a higher volume of applications, and after ensuring that it does not lead to disproportionate delays in obtaining authorisation - which may affect the efficiency of public procurement.

Reconciling regulatory constraints, standards and certifications with a high level of competition in public procurement

Regulatory requirements (technical standards, product certifications and approvals[2]) imposed on suppliers play a key role in public procurement. Their primary aim is to ensure that products and public works undertaken comply with the health, quality or safety requirements of public authorities or minimise the environmental externalities of suppliers' activities.

However, excessive regulatory requirements may reduce the number of potential suppliers, exposing procurement officials to risks of bribery and increasing the risk of collusion between suppliers or for example, between certain producers and installers of equipment in the field of urban infrastructure. These areas of limited competition also expose procurement officials to risks of bribery. These requirements equally contradict the "access" principle of the OECD Recommendation on Public Procurement, which emphasises the need to "*encourage broad participation from potential competitors, including new entrants and small and medium enterprises*".

Lambert-Mogiliansky and Sonin (2006) show that the risks of collusion involving bribery are particularly high when competition is weak and the market is characterised by a small number of medium-sized firms with a comparable cost structure (Lambert-Mogiliansky and Sonin, 2006[9]). This market structure applies to numerous cases of collusion in the construction industry highlighted by the Charbonneau Commission.

For example, the asphalt paving market has resulted in bid-rigging agreements among a small number of suppliers of goods with a comparable cost structure. These collusion practices in Montreal in the 2000s were based on territorial sharing of government contracts among five companies, depending on the location of each asphalt plant. This cartel had ensured profit margins of 30% for the companies involved, well above the industry average of 4-8% (CEIC, 2015[10]). Since then, the Government of Quebec has taken several measures to encourage competition between asphalt mix suppliers, notably by increasing the presence of mobile asphalt plants (Bégin et al., 2016[11]).

However, these regulatory requirements have different characteristics depending on whether they relate to product approval, or standards and certification. Indeed, the purpose of approval is to strictly define the products that a contracting authority may purchase, whereas standards and certifications oblige bidders to demonstrate the conformity of products and services with these requirements. In the former, the market is frozen since only approved products can be acquired, while in the latter situation the market is restricted as the procurement officer defines the characteristics of the products and services provided by the companies. The main consequence of this difference is that the risks of bid-rigging are more present in the purchase of approved products, while the risks of bribery increase in markets requiring specific technical standards or certifications because of weak competition. The solutions provided by the Government of Quebec must, therefore, take these differences into account.

Defining strategies to limit collusion on approved products

In Quebec, public and municipal bodies have the option of approving items "to ensure, before issuing a call for tenders, that the item meets a recognised standard or an established technical specification" (Regulation respecting certain service contracts of public bodies - RCAOP, article 573.1.0.2 of the CTA and 936.0.2 of the MC). Notices of approvals from government agencies are published at least once a year on the SEAO. The list of approved goods is also posted on the SEAO. Any CFT after approval is restricted to approved goods only and may result in a contract of up to 3 years.

The MTQ is the public body that manages the largest number of approval programmes in Quebec. These programmes are designed to ensure the use of reliable, quality products, particularly for the construction and maintenance of road networks, while streamlining the procurement process. Other public bodies (Shared Services Center of Quebec, health-related shared procurement groups) and municipalities also manage their own approval programmes.

Many MTQ approval programmes for very specific products involve only 2 or 3 suppliers located in Quebec[3]. This kind of market structure calls for increased vigilance with regard to the risk of collusion and bribery among clients. Although suppliers from Canadian regions with which Quebec has trade agreements are admitted to the approval programmes, they generally go through distributors or manufacturing agents located in Quebec. The increased vigilance must therefore also extend to these various intermediaries.

Measuring the tangible effects of these strategies and systematically assessing the impact of approval programmes on competition

Nevertheless, the impact of these strategies needs to be assessed to ascertain their relevance. In particular, in practice, few non-Quebec equipment installers or suppliers (foreign or from other Canadian provinces) are currently certified by the MTQ, although it must be noted that these suppliers often call upon Quebec partners or distributors to have their products approved.

The MTQ has strengthened the consideration of competition in its approval processes. A market analysis expert is now a member of the approval committees, and the periodic review of approval programmes currently includes market analysis. The Ministry has a team of eight analysts who carry out work on competition, including a monitoring dashboard based on key indicators.

The MTQ's work extended to all of its contracts, with no apparent prioritisation of approved goods contracts. Only the periodic reviews of approval programmes (once every three years) gave rise to specific assessments of their impact on competition. More regular monitoring of competition was introduced in December 2018, including an annual review of products. The MTQ could continue to strengthen its regular monitoring of competition (establishment of indicators, market studies) within its various approval programmes.

Other public agencies and municipalities that manage approval programmes could also assess their impact on competition, for example by developing a dashboard based on the MTQ model. The systematic presence of a market analysis expert on approval committees could be made mandatory, including in municipalities.

On the other hand, and particularly if the strategies developed do not produce the expected effects, procurement officials also have the option of using specific procurement strategies that can minimise the risks of rigging agreements among bidders. In France, for example, the Union of Public Purchasing Groups (Union des groupements d'achats publics) has implemented certain procurement strategies to limit the risks of collusion in markets with little competition. To this end, framework agreements (task order contracts and delivery order contracts) have been drawn up requiring a degressive distribution of volumes between suppliers according to their ranking following a competitive bidding process. These techniques can be used to minimise the risk of collusion, among other things (OECD, 2017[12]).

Conducting a systematic audit of the risks of collusion within the CFTs of approved goods

The small number of potential suppliers of approved goods increases the risk of them colluding to "share" the market between themselves, which also entails risks in terms of integrity. The AMP or the contracting authorities should conduct a systematic analysis of the risks of collusion in markets for approved goods, including using data from the SEAO. Such an analysis presupposes a greater digitalisation of public procurement, as discussed in Chapter 3. Rolling out electronic bid submission would make it possible, in particular, to collect the data necessary for the systematic analysis of collusion risks, as shown in Box 4.6.

Box 4.6. Automated analysis of cartel risks in public procurement

Korea - System for the analysis of cartel indicators in public procurement

The Korean Fair Trade Commission (FTC) works closely with the government regulators to identify transactions that pose a risk of anti-competitive agreements or cartels. In addition to its traditional tools (reporting by competitors or by one of its members), in 2006 the Bureau developed an automated cartel analysis system based on indicators (Bid-Rigging Indicator Analysis System, BRIAS).

The system uses data from the Korean electronic tendering system (KONEPS). It analyses a dataset including the price of each bid (which is compared to a reference price), the number of bidders, the method of procurement, etc. The system applies a formula that generates a score reflecting the probability of rigging. Beyond a certain threshold, the system suggests that users collect more data on a suspicious procedure. A high threshold may also give rise to an investigation into a specific purchasing process, where appropriate. Each month the system analyses the data collected from KONEPS on the procurement processes of the previous month. For goods and services, the system analyses all processes above USD 423 000, while for public works, all those above USD 4.2 million are screened.

United Kingdom - Cartel detection tool available to contracting authorities

The United Kingdom Competition and Markets Authority *(*CMA) provides a free cartel detection tool for contracting authorities. This tool automatically analyses bids and tender documents received. The system's algorithm uses this data to run empirical tests on bid prices, the number and timing of bids, and the tender documents to generate a 'suspicion score' for each procedure.

Contracting authorities can set up tests based on their knowledge of each specific market and the suppliers involved in the tender. The detailed results of each test are available to users.

Sources: Competitions and Markets Authority, *Cartel screening tool for procurers* (Available at: https://www.gov.uk/government/publications/screening-for-cartels-tool-for-procurers/about-the-cartel-screening-tool#case-study-cornwall-council); (OECD, 2016[13]).

Quebec could draw on these two examples to implement collusion risk analysis tools based on SEAO statistics. In addition, the Government should prioritise the markets for approved goods (or markets comprising approved goods) in the implementation of full digitisation of the entire contract management cycle.

Considering centralisation of municipal approval programmes

The approval of goods by each municipality creates additional costs and delays for suppliers. Indeed, they must prepare approval files for each municipality and make themselves available to take part in possible on-site demonstrations. The multiplicity of registration processes could discourage new entrants and foreign suppliers, or suppliers resident in other Canadian provinces.

Moreover, municipalities do not always have the means and critical mass to conduct competition impact analyses or collusion risk audits. Quebec could therefore examine the advisability of entrusting municipal approval programmes to the centre of expertise under the aegis of the MAMH or the *Société québécoise des infrastructures*. The Shared Services Centre could manage information technology approval programmes. Another option would be to provide for mutual recognition of product approvals among municipalities, or to make it mandatory to register through multi-municipal joint procurement groups, such as those that already exist for medical devices.

This more centralised approval process could attract a larger number of suppliers, as it would allow access to larger procurement volumes. Increasing the number of potential suppliers whose products are registered would discourage collusion schemes between suppliers by stimulating new entrants from neighbouring provinces (such as Ontario) in the case of calls for tenders in the Montreal metropolitan area.

Harmonising standards and certification requirements and encouraging supplier innovation

In Quebec, as in many OECD countries, public bodies and municipalities frequently refer to technical standards and require their suppliers to provide products that are certified as complying with these standards. In Quebec, most of these standards are issued by the *Bureau de normalisation du Québec* (BNQ) or another organisation accredited by the Standards Council of Canada (SCC). Some calls for tenders require suppliers to comply with an American or European standard (EC standards). Public bodies also contribute to the formation of new standards: the *Régie de l'Assurance maladie du Québec* (RAMQ), for example, contributes to the formation of a technical standard for wheelchairs under the aegis of the BNQ.

By facilitating the compatibility of products and services, the adoption of standards normally has a favourable effect on competition as it promotes diversity of supply and allows purchasers to easily compare different products, thus reducing information asymmetries. Standards are also an important element in product innovation, as innovative products certified to technical standards are more readily accepted by consumers and clients (OECD, 2017[14]). However, technical standards may also delay innovation and thus access to new market entrants, particularly in cases where two conditions are met: 1) The installed base (the number of products that are being used) relative to an older standard is significant and 2) An innovative product is not compatible with the old standard. (Forrell, Solaner and Org, 1986[15])

In Canada, the technical standards and certification requirements faced by economic actors may vary from province to province. Many standards and certification requirements have differences that create technical barriers to internal trade (Standards Council of Canada, 2018[16]). In some public procurement contracts, these differences may result in a reduced pool of potential suppliers, creating fertile ground for bid-rigging by suppliers. These agreements increase the risk of bribery among procurement officials.

In order to mitigate the "anti-competitive" impact of regulatory standards and requirements on public procurement, the recommendations below present 3 tools available to the Government of Quebec.

Continuing efforts to harmonise standards and certification requirements within Canada and with Ontario

Canadian provinces are engaged in efforts to harmonise standards and certification requirements, which is one of the objectives of the Canadian Free Trade Agreement (CFTA) that will come into effect in 2017. The Standards Council of Canada is engaged with Canadian industry associations in identifying standards-related barriers to interprovincial trade.

Nonetheless, there is little, if any, participation of suppliers from other Canadian provinces in public procurement processes in Quebec. For example, the *Régie de l'Assurance maladie du Québec* reports that bidders resident in other Canadian provinces do not participate in its CFTs, with technical standards presenting a major barrier. One way to increase the participation of suppliers from other Canadian provinces is through the harmonisation of technical standards and certification requirements among provinces. Harmonisation does not mean the outright adoption of the standards and certification requirements of other provinces, but rather the gradual development of common standards. The Government of Quebec could therefore continue its contribution to the harmonisation of standards and certification requirements at the federal level to remove technical barriers to increased competition in public procurement. Besides, better co-ordination between standards assessment bodies (SAB) and federal, provincial and municipal regulators is needed to avoid the development of non-harmonised requirements in newly regulated sectors (Standards Council of Canada, 2018). The Government of Quebec could contribute to the reconciliation of standardisation requirements as part of the modernisation of the CFTA.

The 2009 Ontario-Quebec Trade and Cooperation Agreement (OQTCA) includes provisions for regulatory co-operation (Chapter 3, including Article 3.6). In the absence of harmonisation at the federal level, the harmonisation of technical standards and certification requirements between Quebec and Ontario, particularly with respect to construction work, can be a powerful tool for increasing competition in public procurement in the Greater Montreal area. For example, a joint committee on regulatory co-operation (Article 3.6 of the OQTCA) could be convened or reactivated between MTQ experts and representatives of the Ontario Ministry of Transportation.

The MTQ, as the main contractor for construction work, recognises technical evaluations of products in other jurisdictions similar to Quebec under three of its approval programmes. This has paid off, with a manufacturer of road marking paint in Ontario being approved by the MTQ since 2017. However, it is the only Ontario manufacturer approved by the MTQ. The Ministry could therefore continue its efforts by initiating a study of Ontario suppliers to identify potential barriers to submitting their products to its approval programmes. The inclusion of a non-response form (which already exists in the CFT files) would provide the Ministry with information on why suppliers from other Canadian provinces are not participating in its approval programmes.

As a result of internal analyses of competition in its procurement markets, and as part of the review of its approval programmes, the Ministry could more frequently recognise comparable Ontario road equipment standards in segments where the level of supplier competition is unsatisfactory. The choice of Ontario makes sense given the province's pool of potential suppliers and its geographical proximity to densely populated areas of Quebec (notably the Montreal metropolitan region). Indeed, Ontario accounts for a significant share (36%) of construction employees in Canada.

In addition to the MTQ, other public bodies such as the RAMQ or the City of Montréal could consider recognising comparable standards and certifications in effect in Ontario in certain instances of public procurement with a low level of competition. In all cases, such recognition would necessarily be subject to a thorough technical examination by the relevant Quebec authority.

Fostering supplier innovation through innovative product evaluation processes and public procurement programmes

Fostering innovation among suppliers is a means of stimulating competition and often of promoting access to public procurement for new entrants (sometimes innovative SMEs), thus increasing the level of competition. The access of new entrants also helps to thwart the administrative corruption schemes that accompany collusion in many tenders. Indeed, the literature (Compte, Lambert-Mogiliansky and Verdier, 2005[17]) demonstrates that facilitating the arrival of new entrants who are not involved in the corruption networks of established actors is a means of restoring fair competition between suppliers.

However, new products or technologies may not meet the established technical standards referred to in CFTs and approval programmes. To foster innovation among suppliers, contracting authorities could set up an evaluation process for new products and new technologies, similar to that practised by the MTQ.[4]

For municipalities that manage approval programmes, the implementation of such a process could be problematic due to a lack of specialised staff and financial resources. For this reason, the implementation of such a process could go hand in hand with the centralisation of approval programmes managed by municipalities.

Public bodies could also engage in a pre-commercial innovation approach, involving the use of research and development services to create innovative products that are adapted to their needs and that can be tested to ensure compliance with the requirements covered by existing standards. The development of these pre-commercial innovations may require a specific government programme, such as the federal government's "Build in Canada" procurement innovation programme (Box 4.7).

Box 4.7. The Build in Canada Innovation Program (BCIP)

The Build in Canada Innovation Program helps innovators move through the final stages of research and development, from the laboratory to the marketplace. The BCIP enables them to test their innovations in an operational environment, within the structures of the Canadian Federal Government.

The BCIP awards public contracts to contractors whose innovations are at the pre-commercial stage through an open, transparent and competitive procurement process. These contracts lead to an operational test phase. The Departments concerned provide contractors with an assessment of the operational performance of their innovative goods and services. In this way, the BCIP enables innovators to enter the market with a positive first experience of using their innovations. With the assistance of the Office of Small and Medium-sized Enterprises (OSME) of Public Services and Procurement Canada (PSPC), the BCIP also informs innovative SMEs on how to participate in Canada's federal procurement.

Source: Country response to (OECD, 2017[18]), "OECD Survey on Strategic Procurement for innovation 2015", in Public Procurement for Innovation: Good Practices and Strategies, Annex C, OECD Publishing, Paris.

Maintaining high levels of performance and quality requirements without unduly restricting competition

In Quebec, regulations allow public bodies to require suppliers to implement a quality assurance system, including an ISO standard. In terms of quality assurance, the standard generally used is ISO 9001: 2015 (ISO 9001: 2008 in its previous version). A comparable system is in place in the area of environmental specifications (the most common is ISO 14001) that may be required of suppliers by contracting authorities, except in the construction field.

However, the public body may opt for an alternative system known as "preferential margins" if it judges that the requirement to comply with ISO standards "unduly reduces competition". The system of preferential margins makes it possible to accept bidders who do not have a quality assurance system that meets the standard. However, it gives an advantage to bidders with compliant quality assurance systems at the tendering stage: their prices are fictitiously reduced by a margin of between 0 and 10% (for award purposes only). The use of a quality assurance system is mandatory in only one case: that of a contract for information technology professional services, with a value exceeding USD 2 million. However, the head of the contracting authority may authorise a waiver of the enforcement of this obligation if he or she considers it appropriate.

OECD field research has shown that public bodies have different practices in requiring ISO-compliant processes of their suppliers.

The implementation of a quality assurance system in accordance with ISO 9001 or an environmental performance system in accordance with ISO 14001 generates costs and requires a significant investment by suppliers' employees. According to the Business Development Bank of Canada, the entire ISO 9001 certification process can take between 8 and 18 months and costs between USD 12 000 to 50 000. The cost of registration checks, usually ranging from USD 2 000 to USD 30 000 per year[5] may be too high for SMEs and new entrants wishing to participate in public CFTs. They can therefore reduce the level of competition in public procurement by restricting the pool of potential suppliers to established actors already holding certificates of conformity to standards.

The Government of Quebec should consider the possibility that contracting authorities may not be able to require compliance with ISO standards for public procurement involving small amounts. Indeed, SMEs and new entrants for whom ISO certification could represent insurmountable costs are generally interested in calls for tenders for lower value contracts.

In cases where the contracting authority deems the reference to an ISO standard indispensable in the context of a procurement process involving lower award amounts, using a system of preferential margins might be preferable. Indeed, this system provides an incentive for all economic operators (including SMEs and new entrants) to comply with ISO quality assurance standards and to obtain their certification from an accredited conformity assessment body without limiting competition.

Adapting bidding deadlines to the reality of the markets to increase participation in calls for tenders

There is a close link between the integrity of the system, the degree of competition in the CFTs and the deadline for submission of bids. When the duration of CFTs is limited, it does not allow for a competitive environment and represents a risk to integrity. In its handbook for public officials involved in public procurement, the World Bank (2014[19]) states that a bidding deadline which is too tight can make it very difficult for regular bidders to prepare sound tender applications, and on the contrary favours the selection of bidders who have bribed the public procurement officials. Furthermore, a deadline that is too short may encourage some bidders to try to obtain insider information before the publication of the CFT in order to better prepare their bids. Such cases have been uncovered in Quebec by the Charbonneau Commission, for example in the case of water meters in Montreal (Faubourg Contrecoeur).

Further adjusting bid submission deadlines according to the size and complexity of the CFTs

Several empirical analyses confirm the link between procurement integrity, bid submission deadlines and the competitive environment in a given CFT. Fazekas, Tóth and King (2016[20]) have shown that tight bid submission deadlines in CFTs are associated with higher indirect indicators of corruption (e.g. share of CFTs with only one bidder or only one compliant bidder). Furthermore, based on data from the European public procurement journal TED between 2009 and 2014, Fazekas and Kocsis (2017[21]) show that "extreme" bidding periods (very short or very long) are positively correlated with the existence of contracts where only one bidder submits an offer, which is symptomatic of corruption risks. Extreme bidding periods are defined on a case-by-case basis according to the rules in force and market practices in the different countries.

Quebec has recently increased the minimum bidding period for certain calls for tenders

Different practices are observed in OECD countries relating to the issue of deadlines for the submission of public procurement bids. For example, a minimum time limit exists in European Union countries, whereas in the United States, federal public procurement rules give greater freedom to public bodies: they only specify that the contracting authority must give bidders sufficient time to prepare their bids.

In Quebec, current regulations prescribe a minimum 15-day submission period for all CFTs from public and municipal bodies. However, contracting authorities may allow a longer period to ensure optimum competition conditions. Following the publication of a CFT, a bidder may also ask the public or municipal body to extend the period. If the organisation accepts, an *addendum* is published on the SEAO and is available to all bidders.

Nevertheless, since 2017, a minimum 30-day bidding period (25 days in the case of electronic bidding) has been stipulated for certain major CFTs covered by the CETA (the Canada-European Union Comprehensive Economic and Trade Agreement): CFTs for goods and services over USD 365 700 and construction contracts over USD 9.1 million[6].

Box 4.8. Minimum bidding time for open tenders

Some OECD countries have included a minimum period for bid submission to open calls for tenders in their regulatory frameworks:

- European Union: Directive 2014/24/EU of the European Parliament and of the Council of 26 February provides that public contracts exceeding the thresholds requiring the use of an open procedure must provide for a minimum bidding period of 35 days. Below these thresholds, the bid submission period is governed by national legislation.
- Australia: federal public procurement rules set a minimum bidding period of 30 days.
- Chile: The Public Procurement Law provides for a minimum 30-day period for calls for tenders from CLP 238 645 000 (USD 375 000).
- New Zealand: article 31 of the Government Rules of Sourcing provides for a minimum of 25 days for open calls for tenders.

Sources: (European Commission, 2014[3]; Australian Government, 2017[22]; New Zealand Government, 2011[23]; Ministry of Finance, Chile, 2004[24]).

At first glance, the minimum periods in Quebec are therefore significantly shorter than those in other jurisdictions (Box 4.8). However, public and municipal bodies have the option of providing longer periods, and this is a relatively common practice as shown in Table 4.2.

Table 4.2. Average period for submission of bids (in number of days) for CFTs

Type of purchases	2015-16	2016-17
Supplies	27	29
Services	24	22
Construction work	24	27
Total	24	25

Note: The average period was calculated based on the difference in days between the launch date and the closing date of the CFT.
Source: Treasury Board Secretariat - SEAO.

Furthermore, since the introduction of the extended minimum period for public procurement subject to the CETA in 2017, the most significant procurement processes are subject to longer submission periods, thus coming closer to international practice for purchases of amounts above the CETA thresholds (see above).

Developing guidelines defining targeted average submission periods according to procurement categories

In terms of deadlines, the central issue is not so much the question of minimum periods as their adaptation to the complexity of the relevant tender. In the case of Quebec, the bid submission periods for some CFTs may not be suitable for the complexity of the bids and the reality of the market, which may increase the risk of integrity violations due to lack of competition.

As shown in Table 4.2 above, average submission periods are generally longer than the minimum 15-day period (Table 4.2), suggesting that contracting authorities were consistently setting longer submission periods, even before the CETA came into effect in 2017. This shows a certain adaptation of bidding periods to the characteristics of each call for tender.

However, the actual bidding periods for construction works appear to be very close to the other procurement categories (services and supplies). For example, in 2015-16, average bid submission periods were 27 days for supply and service contracts and 24 days for construction. When the CETA entered into force in July 2017, it increased the minimum biding period for CFTs to 30 days, thus increasing the average bidding period for CFTs above the threshold. Below the thresholds, however, the submission periods have not changed significantly and remain very similar for the different procedures (26 calendar days for construction works and 23 for service and supplies contracts). Given that the thresholds are much lower for contracts for supplies (USD 365 700) than for construction works (USD 9.1 million), the problem of bidding periods that are too short is particularly acute for construction works. Statistics on the extension of the period for submission of bids during the tender process suggest that the periods for some CFTs may be too short. For example, *addenda* that extend the period for bid submission account for a considerable proportion of CFTs: more than a third (35%) of the CFTs of public bodies have been subject to such an *addendum* for 2016-17, and slightly more than 27% for municipal ones. , the share of CFTs subject to such *addenda* is increasing, accounting for 31% (public bodies) and 22.1% (municipalities) respectively of all CFTs over 2014-15. A number of contingencies may arise that force the government body to rethink its planning. However, these increasingly frequent submission prolongation *addenda* may indicate that the contracting authorities sometimes underestimate the submission period required given the complexity and size of their CFTs.

Accordingly, the Government of Quebec could encourage public bodies and municipalities to further adapt the deadline for submission of bids to the complexity of the CFTs, particularly in the case of construction works. For example, it could develop guidelines defining target average bidding periods for each contracting authority and by purchasing category. This is particularly important since planning for future purchases is only very occasionally published in Quebec, as discussed in more detail in Chapter 2.

Adjusting the target average bidding periods based on the publication of advance information notices and electronic submissions

This report recommends that the Government of Quebec consider the mandatory publication of advance information notices and procurement plans of public and municipal (Chapter 2). Average bidding periods could be shorter in cases where the advance notice of information (via the SEAO) or procurement plans are published. Moreover, this period could be reduced when the public or municipal body requires electronic bid submission. Australia and the EU provide examples of adjustments to the bid submission periods of CFTs based on these criteria (Box 4.9).

Box 4.9. Differentiated submission periods in the European Union and Australia

In the European Union,, the minimum bid submission period is 35 days for open procedures, but it is reduced to 30 days if electronic submission is accepted. It is further reduced to only 15 days if a pre-information notice has been published.

In Australia, federal procurement rules set a minimum bidding period of 25 days for an electronic CFT and 30 days for a non-electronic CFT. However, the bid submission period may be shorter (between 10 and 25 days) if a detailed procurement plan has been published on the electronic procurement platform AusTender between 40 days to one year before the publication of the procurement notice.

Sources: (European Commission, 2014[3]; Australian Government, 2017[22]).

Adjusting the minimum bidding period for Invitations to Tender (ITT)

ITT (Invitation to Tender) is an unpublished procedure that allows contracting authorities to solicit bids from certain suppliers (see Chapter 2). The regulations set a minimum period of eight days for the submission of bids.

This minimum period is shorter than in many other OECD countries (Box 4.9). For example, in New York State, a minimum submission period of 15 days applies to all types of procedures below the CFT threshold. In Chile, the periods for submitting bids in response to private calls for tenders are the same as those for public calls for tenders and depend on the estimated value of the contract (20 days above CAD 89 000 and 10 days above CAD 8 900) and the complexity of the goods and services to be procured.

The Government of Quebec could therefore encourage public and municipal bodies to adapt the submission periods for responding to ITTs based on the complexity and value of the contracts and to apply, where appropriate, the same period as for a CFT (15 days), particularly in the case of construction contracts.

Increasing the 7-day period for addenda impacting on bid prices

Although the periods for submitting bids are, especially for the most complex and costly ones, generally in line with international practice, response times granted to bidders following substantial changes in the tender documentation pose an additional risk of corruption in the public procurement process concerned. In their empirical research on CFTs in Hungary, Fazekas, Tóth and King (2016[20]) found that a bidding period shorter than the legal deadline, in particular where weekends are improperly counted as working days, increases the likelihood that a single bidder will be declared compliant (a bribery risk factor) by about 20%.

Any *addendum* to the tender documents which may affect bid prices (change in technical specifications or quantity) stipulates a minimum 7-day period between its publication and the closing date of the CFT. If necessary, the contracting authority must postpone the deadline of the CFT to comply with this minimum period.

This type of change requires bidders to re-examine their bids, sometimes thoroughly. In France, in the event of a substantial change to an open call for tenders with an impact on price, administrative case law requires the contracting agency to relaunch a new public call for tenders, again respecting the minimum bidding periods.[7] To avoid the risks of bribery inherent in short bid preparation times, the Government of Quebec should increase this period by a further 7 days to bring it closer to the minimum period for the submission of CFTs (15 days).

Action plan

Communication with the private sector

- Maximising the potential of the SEAO for fair and transparent communication with suppliers
- Developing tools to guide interaction with suppliers appropriately during the market research and knowledge acquisition phase

Using enhanced controls on business integrity

- Setting clear and measurable objectives for the contract authorisation regime
- Considering an extension of the contract authorisation regime to more public contracts based on a risk analysis
- Considering the total acquisition cost criterion instead of the price criterion to ensure the true comparability of bids, and establishing a Selection Committee when using the price criterion

Reconciling regulatory constraints with high levels of competition

- Measuring the tangible effects of these strategies and systematically assessing the impact of approval programmes on competition
- Conducting a systematic audit of the risks of collusion in the CFTs of approved goods
- Considering the centralisation of municipal approval programmes
- Continuing efforts to harmonise standards and certification requirements within Canada and with Ontario
- Fostering supplier innovation through innovative product evaluation processes and public procurement programmes
- Maintaining high levels of performance and quality requirements without unduly restricting competition

Adapting bid submission periods to the reality of the markets

- Developing guidelines defining target average bid submission periods according to purchasing typologies
- Adjusting the average target bid submission timeframes based on advance information notices and electronic submissions
- Adjusting the minimum bid submission period for Invitations to tender (ITT) to the complexity and size of the contract
- Increasing the 7-day period for addenda impacting on bid prices

References

Australian Government, D. (2017), *Commonwealth Procurement Rules: Achieving value for money*, https://www.finance.gov.au/sites/default/files/commonwealth-procurement-rules-1-jan-18.pdf. [22]

Bégin, L. et al. (2016), "Rapport du Comité public de suivi des recommandations de la Commission Charbonneau", *Éthique publique* vol. 18, n° 2, http://dx.doi.org/10.4000/ethiquepublique.2789. [11]

CEIC (2015), *Rapport final de la Commission d'enquête sur l'octroi et la gestion des contrats publics dans l'industrie de la construction*, https://www.ceic.gouv.qc.ca/fileadmin/Fichiers_client/fichiers/Rapport_final/Rapport_final_CEIC_Integral_c.pdf. [10]

Champagne, S. (2018), "Plus de concurrence depuis la commission Charbonneau", *La Presse*, http://www.lapresse.ca/affaires/portfolio/ingenieurs-conseils/201802/21/01-5154755-plus-de-concurrence-depuis-la-commission-charbonneau.php. [5]

Compte, O., A. Lambert-Mogiliansky and T. Verdier (2005), *Corruption and Competition in Procurement Auctions*, WileyRAND Corporation, http://dx.doi.org/10.2307/1593751. [17]

European Commission (2014), *Directive 2014/24/UE du Parlement européen et du Conseil du 26 février 2014 sur la passation des marchés publics et abrogeant la directive 2004/18/CE*, http://data.europa.eu/eli/dir/2014/24/oj. [3]

Fazekas, M. and G. Kocsis (2017), "Uncovering High-Level Corruption: Cross-National Objective Corruption Risk Indicators Using Public Procurement Data", *British Journal of Political Science*, pp. 1-10, http://dx.doi.org/10.1017/S0007123417000461. [21]

Fazekas, M., I. Tóth and L. King (2016), "An Objective Corruption Risk Index Using Public Procurement Data", *European Journal on Criminal Policy and Research*, http://dx.doi.org/10.1007/s10610-016-9308-z. [20]

Forrell, J., G. Solaner and E. Org (1986), "Competition, Compatability and Standards: The Economics of Horses, Penguins and Lemmings", Department of Economics, Institute for Business and Economic Research, UC Berkeley, https://escholarship.org/uc/item/48v4g4q1 (accessed on 7 September 2018). [15]

Hjelmeng, E. and T. Søreide (2014), "Debarment in Public Procurement: Rationales and Realization", in Racca, G. and C. Yukins (eds.), *Integrity and Efficiency in Sustainable Public Contracts*, Bruylant, http://doi.org/10.13140/2.1.4950.4645. [2]

Lambert-Mogiliansky, A. and K. Sonin (2006), "Collusive market sharing and corruption in procurement", *Journal of Economics and Management Strategy*, http://dx.doi.org/10.1111/j.1530-9134.2006.00121.x. [9]

Ministry of Finance, Chile (2004), *Reglamento de la ley N° 19.886 de bases sobre contratos administrativos de suministro y prestación de servicios*, https://www.leychile.cl/Navegar?idNorma=230608. [24]

New Zealand Government (2011), *Mastering Procurement: A structured approach to strategic procurement*, https://www.procurement.govt.nz/assets/procurement-property/documents/guide-mastering-procurement.pdf. [23]

OECD (2017), *OECD Integrity Review of Mexico: Taking a Stronger Stance Against Corruption*, OECD Public Governance Reviews, OECD Publishing, Paris, https://dx.doi.org/10.1787/9789264273207-en. [4]

OECD (2017), "OECD Survey on Strategic Procurement for innovation 2015", in *Public Procurement for Innovation: Good Practices and Strategies*, OECD Publishing, Paris, https://dx.doi.org/10.1787/9789264265820-42-en. [18]

OECD (2017), *Public Procurement for Innovation: Good Practices and Strategies*, OECD Public Governance Reviews, OECD Publishing, Paris, https://dx.doi.org/10.1787/9789264265820-en. [14]

OECD (2017), *Public Procurement in Chile: Policy Options for Efficient and Inclusive Framework Agreements*, OECD Public Governance Reviews, OECD Publishing, Paris, https://dx.doi.org/10.1787/9789264275188-en. [12]

OECD (2016), *Improving ISSSTE's Public Procurement for Better Results*, OECD Public Governance Reviews, OECD Publishing, Paris, https://dx.doi.org/10.1787/9789264249899-en. [1]

OECD (2016), *The Korean Public Procurement Service: Innovating for Effectiveness*, OECD Public Governance Reviews, OECD Publishing, Paris, https://dx.doi.org/10.1787/9789264249431-en. [13]

PwC (2014), *Fighting Corruption and Bribery in the Construction Industry*, Engineering and construction sector analysis of PwC's 2014 Global Economic Crime Survey, https://www.pwc.com/gx/en/economic-crime-survey/assets/economic-crime-survey-2014-construction.pdf. [7]

Standards Council of Canada (2018), *Solutions de normalisation pour éliminer les obstacles au commerce canadien*, https://www.scc.ca/fr/system/files/publications/SCC_RPT_Standardization_Solutions_To_Remove_Trade_Barriers_in_Canada-FR.pdf. [16]

VGQ (2018), *Autorisation de conclure des contrats et sous-contrats publics*, Rapport du Vérificateur général du Québec, http://www.vgq.gouv.qc.ca/fr/fr_publications/fr_rapport-annuel/fr_2018-2019-juin2018/fr_Rapport2018-2019-PRINTEMPS-ChapAMF.pdf. [6]

VGQ (2016), *Contrats d'achats regroupés en technologies de l'information*, Rapport du Vérificateur général du Québec, https://www.vgq.qc.ca/Fichiers/Publications/rapport-annuel/2016-2017-VOR-Printemps/fr_Rapport2016-2017-VOR-Chap02.pdf. [8]

World Bank (2014), *Fraud and Corruption Awareness Handbook: A handbook for civil servants involved in public procurement*, World Bank Group, http://documents.worldbank.org/curated/en/309511468156866119/Fraud-and-corruption-awareness-handbook-a-handbook-for-civil-servants-involved-in-public-procurement. [19]

Notes

[1] This refers to shareholders, chief executives and directors.

[2] In Quebec, approval is a procedure for product validation by the contracting authority prior to the publication of the CFT itself.

[3] An example of this is the HOM 5660 - 101 programme “Semi-Rigid Guardrail End Devices”. Under another programme (“Systems for Lighting and Light Signalling Structures” HOM 6310), there are only two approved products, supplied by installers who purchase from the same US manufacturer.

[4] The MTMDET's evaluation process for new products and technologies allows manufacturers of innovative products to submit them for in-depth review. Refer to the Ministry's website for further details on this process: https://www.transports.gouv.qc.ca/fr/entreprises-partenaires/entreprises-reseaux-routier/guichet-unique-qualification-produits/Pages/evaluation-produits-nouvelle-technologie.aspx.

[5] Presentation of the ISO standard on the Bank's website, https://www.bdc.ca/fr/articles-outils/operations/iso-autres-certifications/pages/processus-certification-iso.aspx

[6] Thresholds valid in July 2018, subject to change according to the evolution of exchange rates. The original thresholds are expressed in IMF Special Drawing Rights.

[7] EC, 16 November 2005, Ville de Paris, No 278646. Text of the judgement available at https://www.legifrance.gouv.fr/affichJuriAdmin.do?oldAction=rechJuriAdmin&idTexte=CETATEXT000008223687&fastReqId=1479551974&fastPos=1.

5 The importance of contract performance in detecting, preventing and managing the risks of fraud and bribery in Quebec

This chapter analyses the measures implemented by the Government of Quebec to strengthen the resilience of the performance phase of public procurement to the risks of fraud and bribery. It discusses increasing the attention given by public actors to this critical stage of public procurement. This chapter also identifies additional actions that would allow for greater accountability of all actors in detecting, preventing and managing the risks of fraud and bribery. Finally, this chapter discusses targeted initiatives that would give public actors better insight into the existence of contracts at risk.

Stakeholder accountability for transparent and efficient management of contract performance

While the design and award phases of public procurement are subject to particular attention in many OECD member countries, including Canada and especially Quebec, the vulnerability of the contract performance phase to corruption risks has long been neglected.

Yet, it is in the latter case that the tangible effects of corruption, whatever its origin, become apparent either through poor or suboptimal performance of expected services or through the granting of undue payments. Moreover, some studies suggest that bribery or fraud related to contract performance generate the largest amounts of undue payments (Piga, 2011[1]).

Defining an effective framework to insulate public procurement from corruption risks related to the contract performance phase

In response to cases of corruption in the performance of public procurement and the practices updated in response to the Charbonneau Commission, the Government of Quebec has developed numerous instruments to better insulate public procurement from the risks of corruption affecting the contract performance phase.

Quebec has developed an extensive legislative arsenal

First, the Quebec government has strengthened its legislative arsenal by increasing the number of measures related to monitoring the performance of public procurement to eliminate companies guilty of wrongdoing during the contract performance phase. For example, the Act respecting contracting by public bodies, last revised in 2017, aims, among other objectives related to fairness, transparency and efficiency, to promote the following fundamental principles:

- public confidence in public procurement by demonstrating the integrity of competitors
- implementation of quality assurance systems which cover the supply of goods, services or construction works required by public bodies
- accountability based on the responsibility of the heads of contracting authorities and on the proper use of public funds.

The contract performance phase is therefore of paramount importance as it helps to build public confidence in public procurement and provides the opportunity to implement quality assurance systems and accountability mechanisms. Indeed, achieving these objectives depends on the framework defining the relations between public and private actors during the performance of procurement contracts.

Stakeholder accountability for confirmed acts of corruption in the conduct of public procurement has been widely developed in Quebec. Various laws aiming to create a robust structure for analysing and monitoring public procurement (the 2011 Anti-Corruption Act, the 2012 Integrity in Public Contracts Act, and most recently the Act facilitating oversight of public bodies' contracts and establishing the Autorité des marchés publics of December 2017) have been passed and are applicable to all public procurement.

As of January 2012, the main provisions of the ACPB related to sanctions imposed on companies found guilty of offences in the performance of public procurement contracts also apply at the municipal level. Indeed, both the RENA and, more recently, contract authorisation, are instruments used in municipal public procurement.

They make it possible, as shown in Figure 5.1 below, to identify businesses that have been found guilty of offences relating to the performance of public procurement contracts or where there are serious doubts as to their ability to perform them with integrity and in a satisfactory manner.

Figure 5.1. Number of new RENA registrations per year

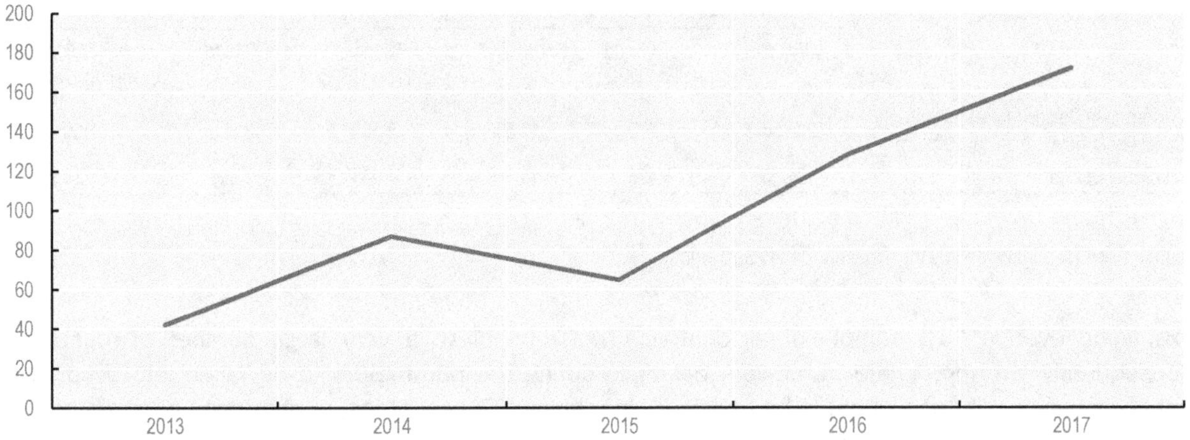

Source: (Treasury Board Secretariat, 2018[2]).

Entities dedicated to the fight against corruption in the contract performance phase should prioritise their efforts

The various legislative reforms have also created independent monitoring and investigative bodies or expanded the powers of existing entities. Many of these actors have, among other tasks, a role in monitoring contractual performance in public procurement. The Charbonneau Commission, in its Recommendation No. 1 on the creation of the AMP and the endowment of extensive powers over public procurement, assigns particular importance to the possibility of assisting contracting authorities in their contractual management, including the performance of contracts entered into by public bodies. More specifically, the functions of the Public Procurement Authority include:

- reviewing, on its own initiative, a contracting process or the performance of a contract, and making recommendations to the public body concerned
- investigating the contractual management of a public body that has been designated by the Authority or the government. In this context, the Authority may make recommendations, terminate a contract or suspend its performance.

Although this increased scrutiny of public procurement is not yet operational (as it is dependent on the AMP CEO taking office), and therefore does not yet have any tangible effects, these successive reforms have all focused on strengthening the integrity of public procurement and creating a more transparent environment.

In addition, some public bodies have also implemented procedures to increase the oversight of public procurement contracts, including their performance. In order to ensure that the tasks of monitoring the enforcement of the statutory framework, verification and control are as efficient as possible and can effectively prevent the risks of bribery, these entities or units (AMP, TBS, Auditor General, BIG, etc.) nevertheless need to ascertain their priorities when it comes to reviews. As shown in Table 5.1 below, an average of 34 343 separate public procurement processes with a value above CAD 25 000 are conducted each year.

These processes sometimes result in several contracts, with 10% being contracts split into lots, or contracts with a performance period exceeding one year. These factors mean that the number of contracts subject to performance monitoring or control concerning transparency and integrity far exceeds the number of procurement processes conducted each year.

Table 5.1. Volume of purchases (in number and value) over the last 3 financial years

	2014-15		2015-16		2016-17	
	Number	Amount (in million USD)	Number	Amount (in million USD)	Number	Amount (in million USD)
Government Bodies (ministries and those under government jurisdiction)	22 756	9 270	19 596	8 533	18 863	9 399
Municipal Bodies	13 973	6 123	14 146	7 241	13 696	6 773

Note: The data for municipal bodies comes from the Electronic Tendering System and has not been validated by the Treasury Board Secretariat.
Source: Information provided by the Treasury Board Secretariat.

Examining even a 10% sample of all contracts would mobilise a very large number of resources. Consequently, an appropriate framework needs to define the parameters to be taken into account in identifying which contracts ought to be reviewed. In many OECD countries, to determine priorities of their audit activities, Supreme Audit Institutions have developed a risk-based methodology (Box 5.1).

Box 5.1. Risk-based audit planning

The approach of Supreme Audit Institutions (SAIs) to audit planning partly depends on their mandate, discretion and independence.

A risk-based approach focuses audit capabilities and efforts on the significant risk areas of the audit environment. For SAIs with an expanded audit mandate, such as Mexico's audit institution *(Auditoría Superior de la Federación*, or ASF), a risk-based approach facilitates the prioritisation of audits and allows for targeted resource allocation based on a qualitative and/or quantitative assessment of the added value of audits.

Risk-based audit planning differs from one SAI to another, but generally involves a process of criteria development, risk identification, risk analysis, risk assessment and mapping, prioritisation and selection of audits; it takes account of the strategic objectives, capabilities and resources of the institution. The criteria can be drawn from different sources, as illustrated by the examples below and may change for different types of audits. For financial audits, material errors in the accounts or financial statements may be the main criterion. For performance audits, the primary criterion may focus more on efficiency, effectiveness and the economic dimension or the extent to which objectives have been achieved.

The following countries have adopted risk-based audit planning:

Belgium

The Belgian Court of Accounts uses a 'Financial Operational Risk Model' (FORM), which is an integrated risk-based planning model. The prioritisation of audits is based on three criteria, one of which is the financial budgetary significance for evaluating the budgetary relevance of the institution on a consolidated level. Budget thresholds are determined taken into account the total federal budget. The second criterion relates to budget priorities and controls. As part of this, the Court considers policies as well as horizontal issues affecting different public entities. The third criterion involves general considerations based on the professional judgement of the Court's management. This criterion receives less weight for programmes with smaller budgets.

Denmark

The Danish Court of Audit *(Rigsrevisionen)* uses a risk-based approach to audit planning. Rigsrevisionen first carries out a strategic analysis of each ministerial level or department. The objective of the analysis is to understand an entity's situation and identify potential risks. This analysis also includes a review of the management of related public bodies. Before the audit is launched, Rigsrevisionen discusses the strategic analysis with the management of the department and the related public body to avoid overlooking important aspects of the audit. The strategic analysis provides a basis for audit planning, which focuses on the identified risk areas/sectors.

Source: Adapted from (OECD, 2017[3]).

As discussed further below, greater harmonisation of the principles defining the relationship between contracting authorities and suppliers, and the definition of standardised indicators, will enable the various institutions in charge of monitoring, control and audit activities to have better awareness of contracts where performance appears to be at risk. Thus a strategic assessment of contracts subject to monitoring, control or audit can be carried out.

The definition and role of the direct actors are only partially taken into account particularly during the contract performance phase

However, these reforms and initiatives focus mainly on strengthening the monitoring of public procurement and less on the active participation of the actors directly involved in public procurement. However, the latter-contracting authorities and suppliers have a leading role in defining procurement procedures and strategies that are resilient to the risks of fraud and bribery.

The OECD Recommendation on Public Procurement (OECD, 2015[4]) assigns a central place to contract performance. Indeed, the transformation of public procurement, initially perceived as deriving from a purely administrative activity, into a strategic tool of public governance, is leading to greater attention on the entire public procurement cycle. Many of the reforms undertaken in OECD countries illustrate this significant change in the approach to public procurement, as illustrated by the mapping developed by New Zealand (Figure 5.2).

Figure 5.2. Approach to public procurement

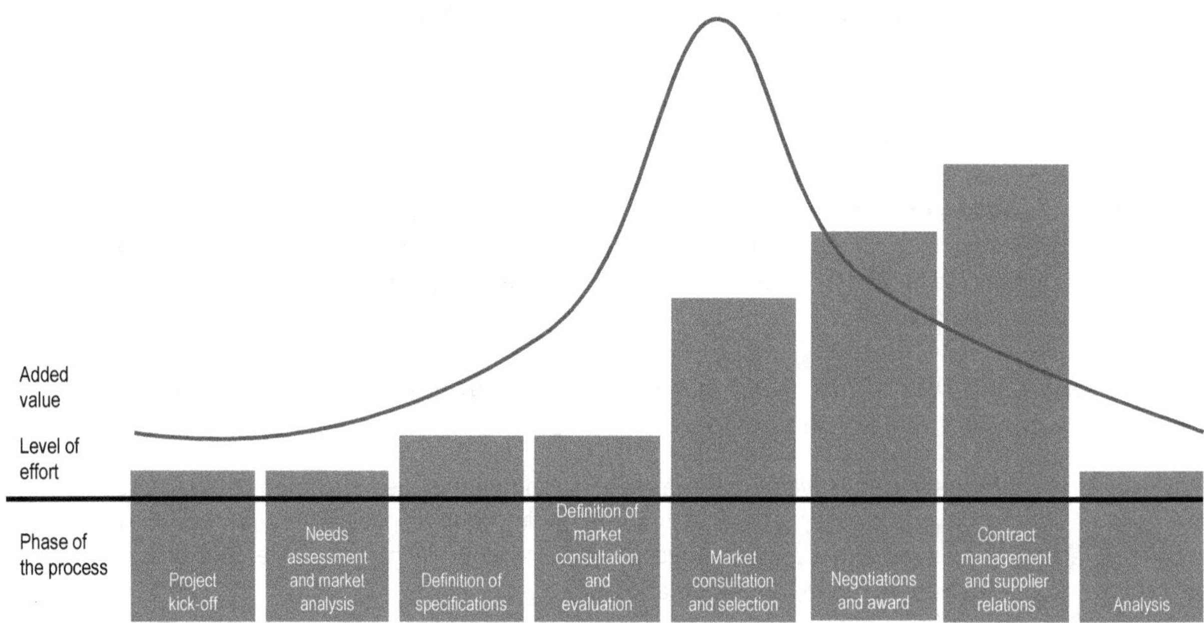

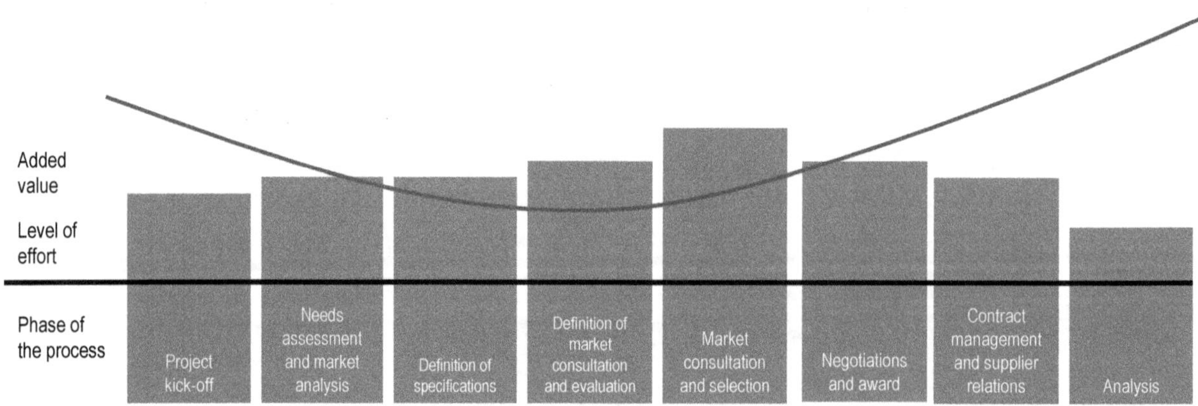

Source: Ministry of Business, Innovation and Employment of New Zealand (2011), *Mastering procurement a structured approach to strategic procurement.*

The primary objective behind strengthening the role of procurement officials in the management of contract performance is ensuring the accountability of the actors directly involved in public procurement, and providing assurance that it produces the expected results. However, this objective is directly threatened by excessive exposure to the risks of corruption. Thus, greater stakeholder accountability is essential to making public procurement more resilient to the risks of corruption.

Harmonising the roles and responsibilities of direct actors in the contract performance phase

The implementation of quality assurance systems and accountability mechanisms is central to the objectives of the ACPB. Nevertheless, the legislative provisions relating to the contract performance phase are brief and deal primarily with the procedures for contractual amendments.

The Regulations specific to certain categories of purchases (Regulation respecting certain supply contracts of public bodies, chapter C-65.1, r. 2; Regulation respecting certain service contracts of public bodies, chapter C-65.1, r. 4; Regulation respecting construction contracts of public bodies, chapter C-65.1, r. 5) provide the general principles applicable to the settlement of disputes related to public procurement contracts but do not detail the role of stakeholders.

In fact, each contracting authority is responsible for drawing up internal guidelines detailing the framework applicable to the management of public procurement, including the performance of contracts. A study by the Treasury Board Secretariat[1] analysing the guidelines of public bodies shows that while some best practices were identified in the sample of contracting authorities selected, they are not systematically applied.

This heterogeneity of practices can be seen, for example, in the description of the role of the officer responsible for the enforcement of contractual rules (RARC), a central figure in each government agency with a leading role in the execution of public procurement contracts. Although some government agencies detail the specific duties of the RARC, the study notes that a number of entities simply refer to the applicable legislative framework.

These differences in the way public procurement operates make the risks of corruption more porous and more difficult to detect. The harmonisation efforts undertaken by the National Health Service (NHS) of Great Britain provide interesting insights into the accountability of actors and their roles in the fight against fraud and bribery (Box 5.2).

Box 5.2. Accountability of stakeholders for combating fraud and bribery in the National Health Service in Great Britain

The National Health Service England (NHS England) has established a comprehensive strategy to combat financial crime, including fraud and bribery. This programme, called NHS Protect, supports the NHS in meeting its commitments as set out in its statutes.

In order to implement these objectives, the programme provides for the introduction of measures to ensure better local accountability and defines the role of the various stakeholders in the fight against fraud and bribery to establish a strategic analysis of these risks.

In support of this programme, the NHS developed an internal policy in 2016 with the following objectives:

- to explain how the NHS intends to combat financial crime
- to provide guidelines for the entire network
- to ensure that the entire system is able to identify financial crimes and understand reporting requirements.

This policy applies to the entire health care system in the United Kingdom including both NHS employees and all those acting in the name and on behalf of the NHS, such as contractors and suppliers.

In July 2018, the NHS Counter Fraud Authority, a body answering directly to the Department of Health and independent of other NHS entities, developed a guide to detecting invoice payment fraud.

Recognising that the practices of the different NHS entities differed substantially in managing contract performance, the guide details the basic principles applicable to invoice processing and sets out the minimum requirements for identifying and preventing fraud risks.

Source: Adapted from (National Health System (NHS), 2016[5]) and (NHS Counter Fraud Authority, 2018[6]).

To consolidate government initiatives and ensure harmonisation of the roles and responsibilities of all actors directly involved in public procurement, the Government of Quebec could develop guidelines that define the roles and responsibilities of the various players and the key elements for identifying and preventing the risks of fraud or bribery.

Reinforcing the responsibility of all those involved in contract performance

Moreover, in some specific situations, other actors play a central role in the performance of public contracts. This is the case, for example, in the construction sector where a private intermediary, often a consulting engineering firm, is responsible for the daily monitoring of the construction site and for validating the progress of the work in accordance with contractual commitments.

To address this specific problem, a practical guide has been developed by the Treasury Board Secretariat (Treasury Board Secretariat, 2018[7]). Although it only briefly deals with the contract performance phase, the guide mentions the importance of ensuring that professional service providers carry out their work under the strict control of contracting authorities. However, several reports by the Quebec Auditor General, including the most recent from2017 (VGQ, 2017[8]), stress the important role of construction site inspectors in public works, and the problem caused by the dilution of responsibilities for contract performance verification.

Existing oversight arrangements such as the contract authorisation that must be obtained for public works contracts over USD 5 million and the resulting sub-contracts, do not apply to site inspectors, who formally have a contract separate to that of the construction company. Furthermore, the thresholds making service contracts subject to a contract authorisation procedure mean that site auditors, although directly related to the construction work, are not subject to the same formalities as the construction company.

The resources and technical expertise needed to monitor projects which are sometimes extremely complex is a problem common to many contracting authorities throughout the world, including in OECD countries. These functions are therefore often partly or entirely outsourced. Also, the more limited the resources of public entities, the more significant this issue becomes. In order to ensure stricter supervision of these activities, the city of Charleston in the United States has developed a specific programme for the accreditation of external inspectors in the field of construction (Box 5.3).

Box 5.3. Building Inspector Certification Programme in Charleston

The City of Charleston Building Inspections Division (BID) Third Party Inspection Program, established in January 2016, is designed to provide a specific framework for the tasks performed by third-party inspectors.

Third-party inspectors must demonstrate that they have the knowledge, skills and abilities to carry out inspections in their area of expertise. Not only must they demonstrate technical knowledge of the law and the trade they are inspecting, they must also demonstrate applicable knowledge of the City's ordinances and by-laws. Among the various elements subject to examination, third party inspectors must be able to demonstrate and maintain their independence from any person or business responsible for the construction of the work they will inspect. The inspector has no personal relationship with the owners, designers, licensees, contractors or subcontractors being inspected. Inspectors cannot have:

1. accepted money or any other item of value other than remuneration from a third party for inspection services; nor
2. performed services or work other than third party inspections on behalf of owners, designers, licensees, contractors or subcontractors inspected for a period of two years prior to performing that inspection.

The programme for the certification of third-party inspectors stipulates an annual review of the conditions for obtaining the certification.

Source: Adapted from (City of Charleston, 2016[9]).

Given the central role of consulting engineering firms in the monitoring and performance of construction work, the Government of Quebec and more specifically the MAMH could consider various possibilities to supervise the activities of site inspectors and ensure that they participate in the honest and transparent conduct of public procurement. Among these options, the Quebec government could consider extending the scope of the authorisation to contract, or of a less onerous procedure, to all contracts directly or indirectly related to those exceeding the established thresholds.

Defining strategic contractual relationships with the private sector: a means of fighting corruption

Using a standardised environment to identify corruption risks during the contract performance phase

Beyond highlighting proven fraudulent practices which emphasise the vulnerability of public procurement, no accurate estimate can be made on the proportion of corruption cases that remain undetected. Nevertheless, since the inherent objective of bribery or fraud is being undetectable, the definition of measures and means to strengthen the resilience of the entire public procurement cycle against potential corruption risks becomes all the more important.

Strengthening the contractual implementation framework by adapting it to the particularities of public procurement

Public procurement is particularly vulnerable to the risks of corruption and some sectors in which procurement officials operate, such as construction or health, are also among the most exposed to business integrity risks. These facts, which were brought to light by the Charbonneau Commission's investigation, are not unique to Quebec, and a report on foreign bribery shows that this problem is common in the construction sector in OECD countries (OECD, 2014[10]).

The evolution of the relationship between the public and private sectors in public procurement is a determining factor which, when taken into account, underlines the importance of implementing standard procedures for the management of contract performance. Indeed, numerous empirical studies (Aminian, Kirkham and Fenn, 2012[11]), (Lonsdale et al., 2010[12]) and (Bovaird, 2006[13])show that the influence of public actors progressively decreases as the delivery of services progresses and the related expenditure increases. This loss of influence increases in line with the complexity of public procurement, as evidenced by the recent reviews of public works and information technology contracts conducted by the Quebec Auditor General (VGQ, 2017[14]).

Figure 5.3. Loss of influence of procurement officials in public works contracts

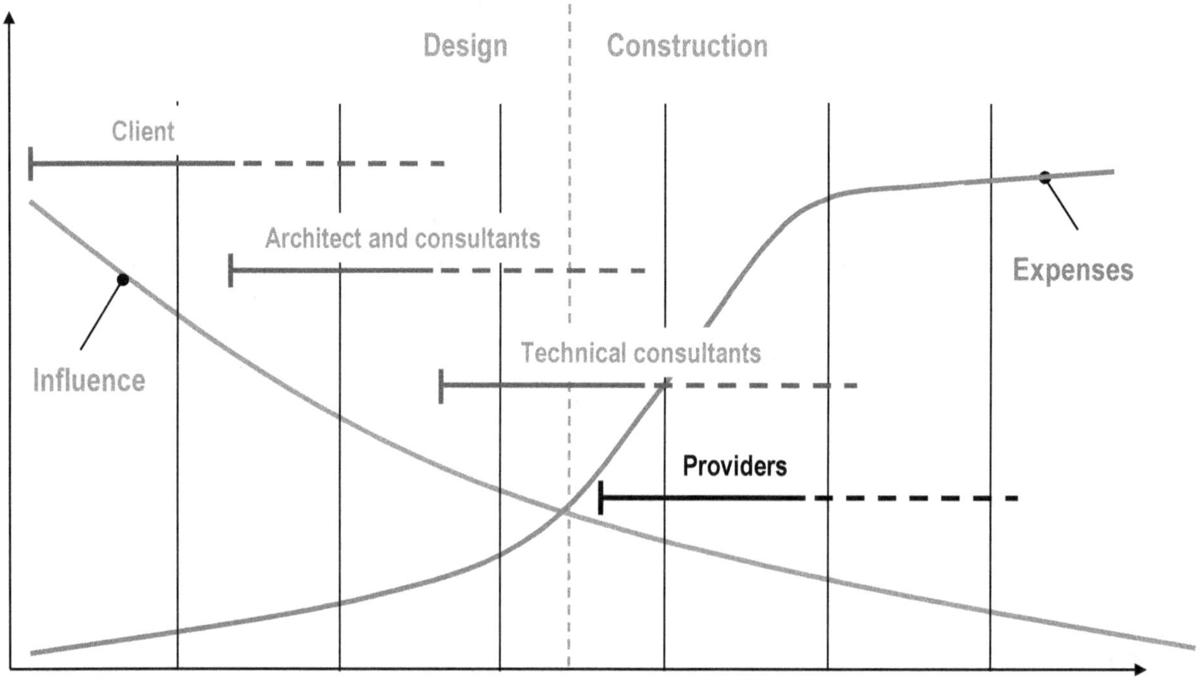

Source: Adapted from (Dale, 2016[15]).

However, susceptibility to corruption risks is also based on the vulnerability of the environment in which stakeholders operate. Indeed, many analyses show that institutional quality is an important variable in exposure to corruption risks (OECD, 2013[16]). In the context of the performance of public procurement contracts, this institutional robustness depends in part on the rules and principles applicable to contractual relations. However, given the brevity of the legislative and regulatory provisions in Quebec dealing with the contract performance phase, these principles are left to the discretion of public bodies and the municipal actors.

In this sense, the development of a comprehensive framework defining the interactions between public actors and suppliers would help to ensure greater resilience to the risks of corruption affecting public procurement. Indeed, an Australian study highlights the benefits achieved by a strategic alignment of values in terms of the efficiency of anti-corruption measures (Australian Commission for Law Enforcement Integrity, n.d.[17]).

The benefits of a strategic alignment of values between procurement officials and suppliers have long been documented, including its impact on organisational efficiency (Barratt, 2004[18]). Nevertheless, ensuring this alignment requires that the contours governing future contractual relationships are identified as soon as acquisition strategies are defined.

Centres of expertise in construction and information technology are currently being set up to support public bodies in these areas, and their creation could be an opportunity to develop a contract management framework adapted to the particularities of these fields.

Taking past performance into account to identify providers at risk

The focal point in defining the contractual relationship between procurement officials and the private sector is the establishment of a framework for evaluating contract performance. In many OECD countries this evaluation is not limited to judging whether or not the objectives defined in the contract have been achieved, but also more broadly the contractors' relationship with the public sector, including its business ethics and integrity.

The Office of Federal Procurement Policy (OFPP) in the United States, for example, has established guidelines for all federal procurement officials to assess and report on the performance and integrity of contractors in public procurement. (Office of Federal Procurement Policy, 2013[19]).

Box 5.4. Evaluating past performance and integrity in the United States

Federal law generally requires agencies to evaluate and document contractor performance on contracts or purchase orders whose value exceeds the simplified acquisition threshold (typically USD 150 000). The evaluation generally focuses on the quality of the product or service provided by the contractor, the contractor's efforts to control costs, timeliness and adherence to schedules, management or business relationships, performance in subcontracting to small businesses, and other applicable factors such as tax crimes.

The performance evaluation and the contractor's response, if any, are stored in government databases, including the Federal Awardee Performance Integrity Information System (FAPIIS), and can be used in future procurement decisions. Among other things, the FAPIIS must contain brief descriptions of civil, criminal and administrative proceedings involving federal contracts that have resulted in a conviction.

In addition, agencies are required by law to consider whether the contractor has a "satisfactory performance record" when determining whether the contractor is sufficiently "accountable" to be awarded a federal contract. The satisfactory performance record includes elements related to the evaluation of the contractor's ethics, such as timely payment to subcontractors. Agencies generally cannot award a contract without first determining that the contractor is "responsible".

Source: Adapted from (Manuel, 2015[20]).

All the Regulations in Quebec include a requirement for the public body to record the evaluation of a supplier whose performance is considered unsatisfactory in a report. This negative evaluation allows the public body to reject the supplier in any new tender procedure. The only notable exception is the evaluation of supplier performance in IT-related public procurement where a comprehensive performance evaluation is required. In addition, as of 1st June 2016, the Regulation respecting contracts of public bodies in the field of information technologies (RCTI) requires public bodies to record an evaluation report of the service provider when the total amount paid for an information technology contract is greater than or equal to USD 100 000.

However, regardless of the content of these reports, for the time being, they are not shared with other public bodies. The consequence is that another public body will not be able to use the experience gained in the performance of previous contracts when identifying eligible providers in its own competitive procedures. This situation will likely change in the near future as the ACPB stipulates the centralisation of the evaluation process under the auspices of the AMP. Nevertheless, an implementing decree is necessary for this provision to be effective.

Given the importance of identifying suppliers who demonstrate integrity and efficiency in the performance of public procurement contracts, the Government of Quebec could ensure that this new provision comes into force as quickly as possible. Consequently, evaluations of unsatisfactory performance can be disseminated to all public and municipal bodies and past performance can be taken into account when awarding public contracts.

Nevertheless, to avoid too much discretion in the debarment of a provider from public contracts, minimum conditions must be defined so that a performance evaluation can be used in future procedures.

The Government of Quebec can draw inspiration from practices implemented in Europe, where the European Union Directive of 2014 stipulates that the past performance of a service provider may be taken into account when excluding a bidder from a tendering process, provided that the poor performance was significant or persistent. This last point implies that the poor performance must have been identified in more than one public procurement process.

Alternatively, the Government of Quebec can look to practices in the United States, where a supplier's past performance is not a reason for debarment but an element in the evaluation of bids. The main effect of this approach is to encourage bidders to improve their practices and their integrity in the performance of contracts, which will then be taken into account in future evaluations. Moreover, this approach has the advantage of not limiting competition since it does not *de facto* exclude a service provider.

Building a resilient environment by analysing and addressing elements of public procurement that impact on corruption risks

Based on a structured and harmonised framework, the effective detection and prevention of corruption in public procurement is only possible if data on contract performance are collected, stored in a structured way and accessible for analysis (PwC, Ecorys, 2013[21]).

Defining risk indicators based on contractual performance

Authorising amendments to public procurement contracts is a practice inherent in any public procurement system. Although signing amendments does not as such provide proof of corrupt acts, it may be symptomatic of the risk of corruption (Racca and Perin, 2013[22]). These acts often take the form of additional expenditure, an extension of the deadline for the performance of services, or a reduction in the scope of services which was not included in the original contract.

Article 17 of the ACPB, like article 573.3.0.4 of the Cities and Towns Act, states that an amendment may be made to a contract as long as it is incidental to the contract and does not change its nature. On the other hand, an amendment does not require authorisation if it is due to a variation in the amount to which a predetermined percentage is to be applied or to a variation in quantity for which a unit price has been agreed.

Amendments to public contracts are subject to publication on the SEAO if they involve additional expenditure which represents more than 10% of the original contract value. Therefore, this factor facilitates the collection of data on this category of amendments. For example, a study conducted in 2013 on the contractual management of certain Quebec public bodies between 2010 and 2013 (KPMG and SECOR, 2013[23]) has shown, that the construction sector in Quebec has seen an increase in contract amendments resulting in additional expenditure. The study establishes the importance of analysing additional expenditure in identifying situations prone to corruption risks.

Nevertheless, as discussed in Chapter 2 of this report, changes to public procurement contracts with respect to an increase in the amount paid to the contractor are not the only indicator of potential corruption risks.

Indeed, as part of a risk analysis, the frequency of contract modifications, and the nature and identity of stakeholders can provide valuable additional indications on the existence of that risk. In addition, these elements provide objective information for comparison that complement the more traditional perception-based indicators (Fazekas and Kocsis, 2017[24]).

In addition to amendments to public procurement contracts with defined prices and scope, expenditures on open contracts, such as task order contracts and delivery order contracts, can provide additional indications of risks of fraud.

These contracts, which represent almost 25% of the total amount of public procurement contracts for government agencies, are not subject to systematic and centralised monitoring. Yet, due to their type and main characteristics, open contracts present specific risks of collusion or bribery (Albano and Nicholas, 2016[25]).

In fact, they offer the flexibility for contracting authorities to place one-off orders with identified suppliers. The lack of monitoring of the amounts actually spent prevents the detection of possible fraudulent schemes. For example, an analysis of spending on certain categories of pharmaceuticals by the decentralised entities of Mexico's Social Security Institute (Instituto Mexicano de Seguro Social, IMSS), the largest health organisation in Latin America, revealed a vast system of collusion (OECD, 2013[26]).

One of the powers attributed to the Autorité des marchés publics (AMP), based on the recommendations of the Charbonneau Commission, is the creation of a team of experts. The Authority has to monitor public contracts to analyse market trends and the contractual practices of public bodies and to identify problem situations affecting competition. During the monitoring or within its verification or investigation work, if the Authority detects indications of embezzlement or the presence of cartels, the LAMP has to send this information to the Anti-Corruption Commissioner, who is responsible for conducting criminal investigations in this area.

The Authority could therefore take advantage of the establishment of this team of experts to define the relevant indicators to help identify the contracts whose performance presents risks of fraud or bribery. As discussed above, these indicators could, in addition to expenditure increases, capture information related to the frequency of contractual amendments, their nature or the identity of stakeholders. They could also provide a general analysis of the final amounts actually spent on the different types of contracts and evaluate these in relation to the original estimates established by public bodies and the municipal actors.

Mitigating some factors that weaken the resilience of the system

An inherent element of public procurement contracts, which may have an indirect effect on the vulnerability of certain contracts to the risks of fraud and bribery, is the question of payment periods. This was particularly highlighted by the Charbonneau Commission. During their testimony before the Commission, several contractors mentioned the problem of delays in the payment of invoices submitted to contracting authorities. Generally, invoices are payable 30 days after the invoice date, but actual payment terms in the construction industry were reported to be 3 to 6 months, according to the contractors.

Beyond its impact on competition in public procurement, this situation involves two specific issues that may have an impact on the vulnerability of public procurement contracts to the risks of fraud and bribery. First, it gives significant power to site supervisors, since they must approve progress payments, among other things. Depending on the speed of their approval, these professionals may either intimidate or be too favourable towards construction contractors, thereby contributing to private bribery schemes.

Second, it permits the infiltration of organised crime into the construction industry. Indeed, an SME facing financial difficulties due to overly large accounts receivable could be tempted to resort to non-legitimate sources of financing. According to the Commission, illegitimate or non-traditional financing is used by a significant proportion of construction companies due to delayed payments. Different OECD countries have implemented specific strategies to accelerate payment terms in their public procurement contracts, especially by targeting specific sectors or types of suppliers such as SMEs (Box 5.5).

Box 5.5. Reducing payment terms in public procurement

The issue of payment terms and their impact on the cash flow of companies holding public contracts is a common concern in many OECD countries. Some countries have established general rules on maximum payment terms applicable to all public procurement contracts, while others have decided to focus their efforts on certain categories of suppliers, particularly SMEs.

France

Decree No. 2013-269 of 29 March 2013 on combating late payment in public procurement contracts, partly codified by the French Public Procurement Code which entered into force on 1 April 2019, standardises the law applicable to all public procurement contracts and increases the penalties for late payment by public authorities. All public contracts have to respect the following deadlines:

1. 30 days for the contracting authorities, including when they act as the awarding entity.
2. 50 days for public health institutions and military health service establishments.
3. 60 days for public enterprises within the meaning of Article 1.II of ordinance n° 2004-503 of June 7, 2004 transposing directive 80/723/EEC on the transparency of financial relations between Member States and public enterprises, with the exception of those considered to be local public establishments.

The payment period, which also applies to subcontractors receiving direct payment, runs from the date of receipt of the payment request or, for the remaining balance of public procurement contracts, from the date of receipt of the final invoice.

United States

The Office of Management and Budget (OMB) Accelerated Payment Policy was initially implemented by OMB Memorandum M-11-32, "Accelerated Payments to Small Businesses for Goods and Services", issued on 14 September 2011. The memorandum states that, to the fullest extent permitted by law, agencies should expedite payments to small business contractors to make payments within 15 days of the receipt of relevant documents.

On 11 July 2012, the OMB took a further step under Memorandum M-12-16, "Providing Prompt Payment to Small Business Subcontractors". Memorandum M-12-16 states that "agencies should, to the fullest extent of the law, temporarily accelerate payments to all principal contractors, to allow them to provide prompt payments to small business subcontractors". The OMB also initially required federal agencies to provide six-monthly reports on their progress in meeting the accelerated payment targets, however later increased the reporting frequency to three months.

Since the inception of the programme in 2011, results have been positive and payment terms for many small subcontracting companies have been reduced from 30 to less than 15 days. In order to make these policies permanent a bill was submitted to the House of Representatives in March 2018.

Source: Adapted from (Ministry of Economy, France, 2013[27]) and (National Small Business Association, 2017[28]).

To address this problem, the recent AMP Act specifically provides that the President of the Treasury Board may, by decree, authorise the implementation of pilot projects to test various measures designed to facilitate payment to companies that are parties to public procurement contracts as well as to related public sub-contracts determined by the Treasury Board, and to define applicable standards in this regard.

Given the impact of delayed payments on the entire supply chain, Quebec could adopt a more systematic response to this issue to minimise its impact. This response could involve rolling out reduced payment terms applicable to all public procurement contracts or a gradual schedule focusing primarily on SMEs, as the most affected category.

Action plan

Stakeholder accountability

- Entities dedicated to the fight against corruption in the contract performance phase should focus their priorities
- Developing tools to guide interaction with suppliers appropriately during the market research and knowledge acquisition phase
- Harmonising the roles and responsibilities of principal actors in the contract performance phase
- Reinforcing the responsibility of all those involved in contract performance

Defining strategic contractual relationships with the private sector

- Strengthening the contractual implementation framework by adapting it to the particularities of public procurement
- Taking past performance into account to identify risky suppliers
- Defining risk indicators based on contractual performance
- Mitigating some factors that weaken the resilience of the system

References

Albano, G. and C. Nicholas (2016), *The Law and Economics of Framework Agreements: Designing Flexible Solutions for Public Procurement*, Cambridge University Press, http://www.cambridge.org (accessed on 20 July 2018). [25]

Aminian, E., R. Kirkham and P. Fenn (2012), *Decreasing Opportunistic Behaviour through Appropriate Contracting Strategies in Construction Industries*, http://www.irbnet.de/daten/iconda/CIB_DC25701.pdf (accessed on 30 July 2018). [11]

Australian Commission for Law Enforcement Integrity (n.d.), *Values alignment*, https://www.aclei.gov.au/corruption-prevention/key-concepts/values-alignment (accessed on 24 June 2018). [17]

Barratt, M. (2004), "Understanding the meaning of collaboration in the supply chain", *Supply Chain Management: An International Journal*, Vol. 9/1, pp. 30-42, http://dx.doi.org/10.1108/13598540410517566. [18]

Bovaird, T. (2006), "Developing New Forms of Partnership With the 'Market' in the Procurement of Public Services", *Public Administration*, Vol. 84/1, pp. 81-102, http://dx.doi.org/10.1111/j.0033-3298.2006.00494.x. [13]

City of Charleston (2016), "Third Party Inspection Program Policy", http://www.charleston-sc.gov/DocumentCenter/View/12847 (accessed on 24 July 2018). [9]

Dale, E. (2016), *Collaboration in the supply chain*. [15]

Fazekas, M. and G. Kocsis (2017), "Uncovering High-Level Corruption: Cross-National Objective Corruption Risk Indicators Using Public Procurement Data", *British Journal of Political Science*, pp. 1-10, http://dx.doi.org/10.1017/S0007123417000461. [24]

KPMG and SECOR (2013), *Revue indépendante de la gestion contractuelle des dépenses supplémentaires associées à des contrats de construction et de services de certains organismes publics Québécois*, https://www.tresor.gouv.qc.ca/fileadmin/PDF/Nouvelles/RapportKPMG_SECOR.pdf (accessed on 24 June 2018). [23]

Lonsdale, C. et al. (2010), "Supplier Behaviour and Public Contracting in the English Agency Nursing Market", *Public Administration*, Vol. 88/3, pp. 800-818, http://dx.doi.org/10.1111/j.1467-9299.2010.01846.x. [12]

Manuel, K. (2015), *Evaluating the "Past Performance" of Federal Contractors: Legal Requirements and Issues*, Congressional Research Service, https://fas.org/sgp/crs/misc/R41562.pdf (accessed on 26 July 2018). [20]

Ministry of Economy, France (2013), "Les délais de paiement dans les contrats de la commande publique", https://www.economie.gouv.fr/files/files/directions_services/daj/marches_publics/textes/autres-textes/fiche-decret-delais-paiement.pdf (accessed on 30 July 2018). [27]

National Health System (NHS) (2016), *Tackling Fraud, Bribery & Corruption: Policy & Corporate Procedures*, https://www.england.nhs.uk/wp-content/uploads/2013/11/frd-brib-corr-pol.pdf (accessed on 24 July 2018). [5]

National Small Business Association (2017), *Feds Prompt Payment Policy Expiring*, http://nsba.biz/feds-prompt-payment-policy-expiring/ (accessed on 30 July 2018). [28]

NHS Counter Fraud Authority (2018), *Invoice fraud guidance for prevention and detection*, https://cfa.nhs.uk/resources/downloads/guidance/NHSCFA%20Invoice%20fraud%20guidance%20-%20v1.0%20July%202018.pdf (accessed on 24 July 2018). [6]

OECD (2017), *Brazil's Federal Court of Accounts: Insight and Foresight for Better Governance*, OECD Public Governance Reviews, OECD Publishing, Paris, http://dx.doi.org/10.1787/9789264279247-en. [3]

OECD (2015), *OECD Recommendation of the Council on Public Procurement*, OECD, Paris, https://www.oecd.org/gov/public-procurement/OECD-Recommendation-on-Public-Procurement.pdf. [4]

OECD (2014), *OECD Foreign Bribery Report: An Analysis of the Crime of Bribery of Foreign Public Officials*, OECD Publishing, Paris, https://dx.doi.org/10.1787/9789264226616-en. [10]

OECD (2013), "Issues paper on corruption and economic growth", https://star.worldbank.org/sites/star/files/oecd_issues_paper_on_corruption_and_economic_growth_2013.pdf (accessed on 25 July 2018). [16]

OECD (2013), *Public Procurement Review of the Mexican Institute of Social Security: Enhancing Efficiency and Integrity for Better Health Care*, OECD Public Governance Reviews, OECD Publishing, Paris, https://dx.doi.org/10.1787/9789264197480-en. [26]

Office of Federal Procurement Policy (2013), *Improving the collection and use of information about contractor performance and integrity*, https://www.acq.osd.mil/dpap/policy/policyvault/USA001513-13-DPAP.pdf (accessed on 20 July 2018). [19]

Piga, G. (2011), "A fighting chance against corruption in public procurement?", *International Handbook on the Economics of Corruption*, Vol. 2, http://www.gustavopiga.it/wordpress/wp-content/uploads/2012/01/Ch5.pdf (accessed on 24 June 2018). [1]

PwC, Ecorys (2013), *Identifying and Reducing Corruption in Public Procurement in the EU*, https://ec.europa.eu/anti-fraud/sites/antifraud/files/docs/body/identifying_reducing_corruption_in_public_procurement_en.pdf (accessed on 23 July 2018). [21]

Racca, G. and R. Perin (2013), "Material Amendments of Public Contracts during their Terms: From Violations of Competition to Symptoms of Corruption", *European Procurement and Public Private Partnership*, Vol. 8/4, http://papers.ssrn.com/sol3/pa- (accessed on 20 July 2018). [22]

Treasury Board Secretariat (2018), *Balises à l'égard des exigences et des critères contractuels en services profesionnels liés à la construction*, https://www.tresor.gouv.qc.ca/fileadmin/PDF/faire_affaire_avec_etat/Balise_construction_services_professionnels.pdf (accessed on 24 July 2018). [7]

Treasury Board Secretariat (2018), *Entreprises inscrites au RENA*, https://rena.tresor.gouv.qc.ca/rena/rechercher.aspx?type=lettre&lettre=a-z (accessed on 27 July 2018). [2]

VGQ (2017), "Audit particulier (partie 2). Ministère des Transports, de la Mobilité durable et de l'Électrification des transports : gestion contractuelle", in *Rapport du Vérificateur général du Québec à l'Assemblée nationale pour l'année 2017-2018*, http://www.vgq.gouv.qc.ca/fr/fr_publications/fr_audit-particulier-enquete/fr_Rapport2017-2018-MTMDET-partie-2/fr_Rapport2017-2018-MTMDET.pdf. [8]

VGQ (2017), "Rapport du Vérificateur général du Québec à l'Assemblée nationale pour l'année 2016-2017", http://www.vgq.gouv.qc.ca/fr/fr_publications/fr_rapport-annuel/fr_2016-2017-Hiver/fr_Rapport2016-2017-HIVER-Chap05.pdf (accessed on 22 June 2018). [14]

Note

[1] Treasury Board Secretariat Analysis Report on Internal Guidelines, July 2016.

www.ingramcontent.com/pod-product-compliance
Lightning Source LLC
LaVergne TN
LVHW081633120826
845149LV00024B/1706

* 9 7 8 9 2 6 4 3 0 5 9 3 9 *